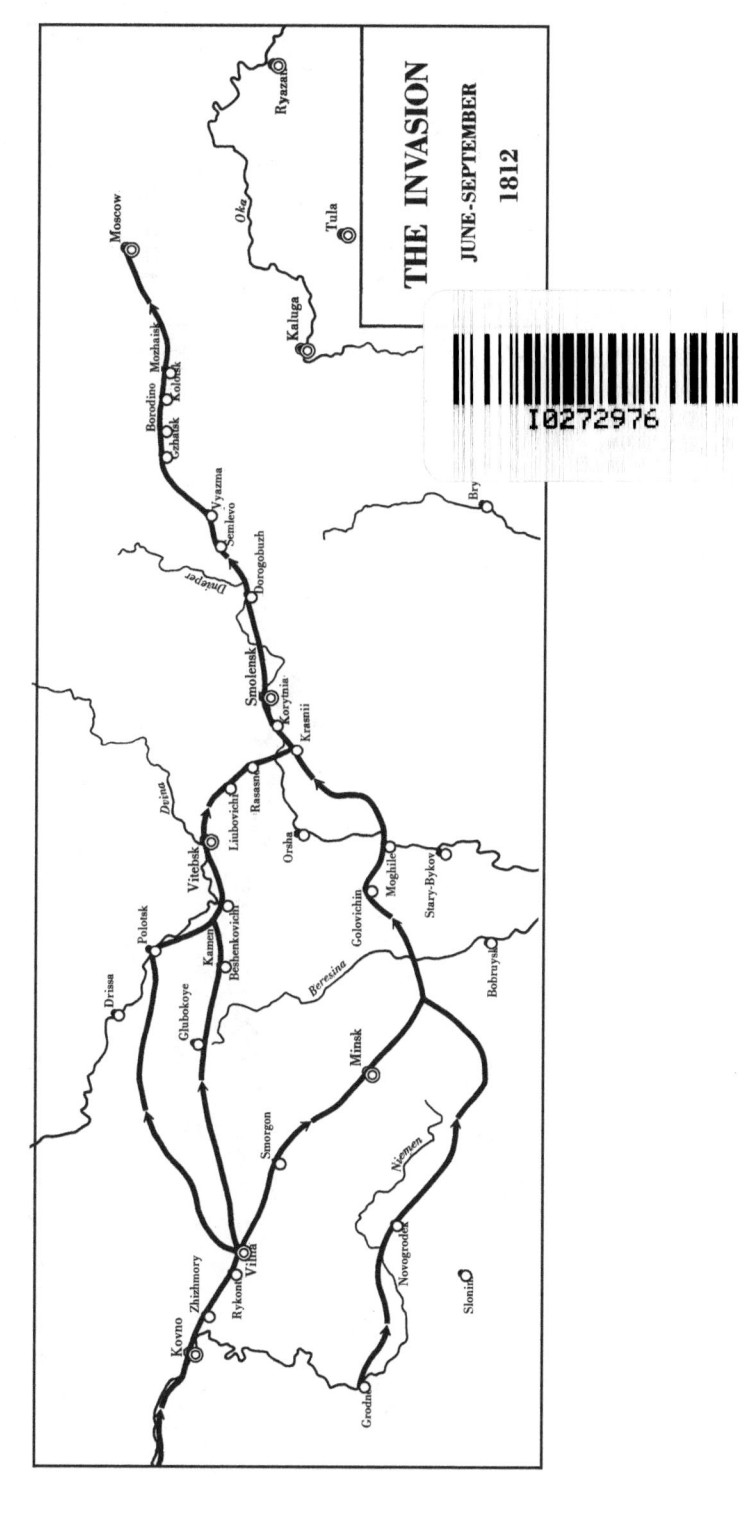

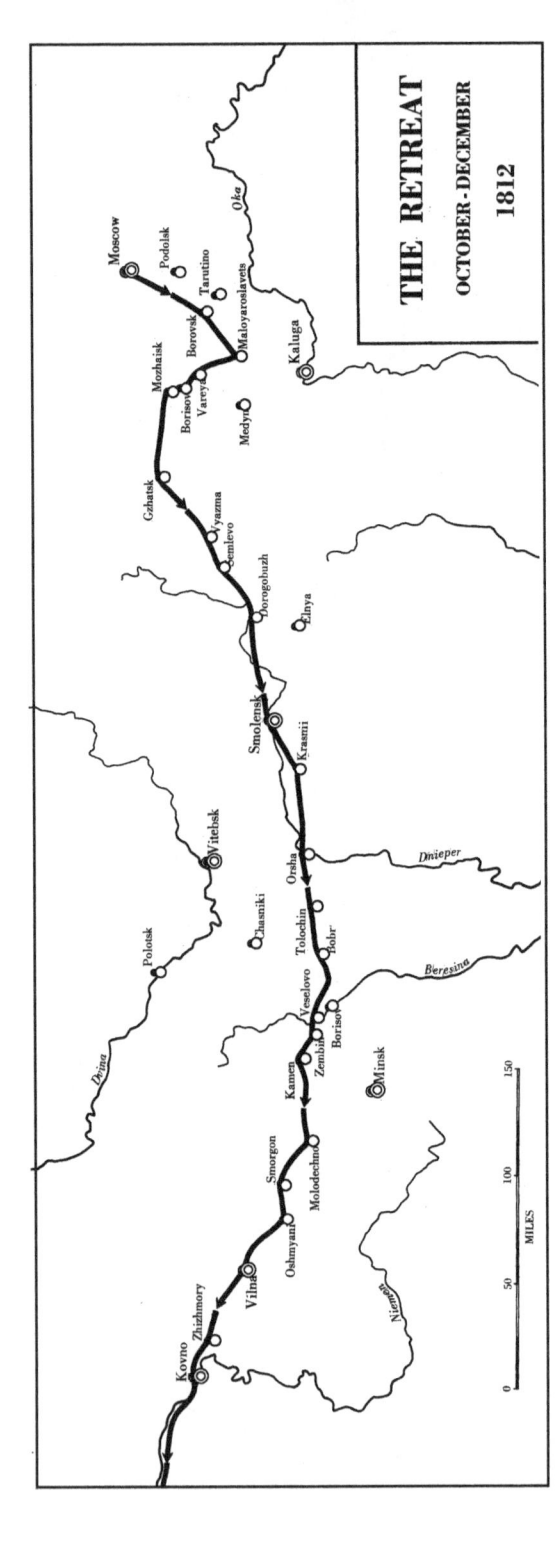

THE RUSSIAN CAMPAIGN, 1812

THE RUSSIAN CAMPAIGN, 1812

by M. de Fezensac

Translated by
Lee Kennett

THE UNIVERSITY
OF GEORGIA PRESS
ATHENS

Paperback edition, 2009
© 1970 by the University of Georgia Press
Athens, Georgia 30602
www.ugapress.org
All rights reserved
Printed digitally in the United States of America

The Library of Congress has cataloged
the hardcover edition of this book as follows:
Library of Congress Cataloging-in-Publication Data

Fezensac, Raymond-Aymery-Philippe-Joseph de Montesquiou, duc de, 1784–1867.
The Russian campaign, 1812, by M. de Fezensac.
Translated by Lee Kennett.
xi, 147 p. map (on lining papers) 23 cm.
ISBN 0-8203-0246-5
Translation of Journal de la campagne de Russie en 1812.
1. Napoleon I, Emperor of the French, 1769–1821—Contemporaries.
2. Napoleonic Wars, 1800–1815—Campaigns—Russia—Personal narratives, French. I. Kennett, Lee B., tr.
DC235 .M65133
940.2'7   70-90563

Paperback ISBN-13: 978-0-8203-3441-7
ISBN-10: 0-8203-3441-3

CONTENTS

INTRODUCTION   VII

PREFACE   XI

PART ONE, CHAPTER ONE   3

The French and Russian armies . . . Declaration of war . . . Passage of the Niemen . . . Headquarters at Vilna . . . The two Russian corps . . . Conquest of all Lithuania . . . Headquarters at Glubokoye . . . Movements of the Russians . . . Combats before Vitebsk . . . Taking the town . . . Cantonments

PART ONE, CHAPTER TWO   18

Stay at Vitebsk . . . Situation of the army . . . March on Smolensk . . . Taking the city . . . Affair at Valutino . . . The Emperor's Plans . . . March on Moscow . . . Battle of the Moscowa

PART TWO, CHAPTER ONE   37

Situation of the Third Corps . . . March from Mozhaisk to Moscow . . . Burning of the city . . . Position of the Third Corps . . . Entry into Moscow . . . Movements of the Russians . . . At Bogorodsk . . . Review of 18 October . . . Order for departure

PART TWO, CHAPTER TWO   50

Plans of the Emperor . . . Departure from Moscow . . . March to Borovsk . . . Operations of the other corps . . . Combat at Maloyaroslavets . . . Retreat toward Smolensk . . . March from Borovsk to Mozhaisk . . . From Mozhaisk to Vyazma . . . Situation of the army . . . Affair at Vyazma

PART TWO, CHAPTER THREE 58
Assigned to the rear guard ... Departure from Vyazma ... March to Dorogobuzh ... Affair at Slopnevo ... Intense cold ... Arrival at Smolensk ... Operations of the other corps

PART TWO, CHAPTER FOUR 69
Departure of the army ... Conduct of Marshal Ney ... Fighting in the suburbs ... Devastation of the city ... Departure of the Third Corps ... Affairs at Krasnii ... Separated from the rest of the army ... Arrival at Krasnii

PART TWO, CHAPTER FIVE 77
Route to Krasnii ... Daring plans of Marshal Ney ... Passage of the Dnieper ... March on the right bank ... Critical state of the regiment ... Arrival at Orsha

PART TWO, CHAPTER SIX 88
Movements of the other corps ... Disorganization of the army ... March to Veselovo ... Movements of the Russian armies ... Reunion of the grand army ... Passage of the Beresina ... Affair of 28 November

PART TWO, CHAPTER SEVEN 98
First days of march ... Difficulties with the rear guard ... Movements of the Third Corps ... Departure of the Emperor ... Renewed intensity of the cold ... Arrival of the army at Vilna

PART TWO, CHAPTER EIGHT 108
State of the army in Vilna ... Withdrawal of the King of Naples ... Attack of the Russians ... Hastened departure ... Charged with the rear guard ... March to Kovno

PART TWO, CHAPTER NINE 115
Situation at Kovno ... Defense of the town ... Passage of the Niemen ... Last attack of the Russians ... Ney's presence of mind ... March to Koenigsberg ... Cantonments on the Vistula ... Arrival at Marienburg

PART TWO, CHAPTER TEN 123
Sojourn on the Vistula ... Defection of the Prussians ... Retreat to the Oder ... Disbanding the army ... Results of the campaign ... Conclusion

APPENDICES 131

INDEX 141

INTRODUCTION

NAPOLEON'S RUSSIAN CAMPAIGN was unquestionably the most decisive military event in the quarter century of war which ended in 1815. The vastness of the enterprise, the fateful consequences which hung upon its success or failure, and the irreparable disaster which finally engulfed it have drawn the interest of generations of military historians.

The events of 1812 also offer to the general reader some of the highest drama to be found anywhere in the pages of modern history. The spectacle which was presented to Europe and the world in June of that year was indeed an impressive one. If a few astute observers had detected that Napoleon's star no longer shone quite so brightly, he was still the greatest military genius of the age. Now he was preparing to humble the last monarch on the continent who still opposed his will. Once Czar Alexander I had accepted the yoke, all Europe would acknowledge Paris as its capital, or so Napoleon fondly hoped. The Grand Army ranged along the banks of the Niemen was perhaps the most imposing military force the world had ever seen. The events which were acted out

Introduction

on the plains of Russia during the ensuing months are the stuff of a Greek tragedy. The enterprise began brilliantly, indeed too brilliantly; and when the good omens became bad ones Napoleon, supreme egoist that he was, ignored their significance until he and his host were completely and irrevocably committed to an undertaking that was doomed. Never did the gods punish hubris more severely.

M. de Fezensac seems to have sensed the timeless grandeur of the tragedy of 1812, for he prefaces his work with a quotation from Virgil's *Aeneid*: "O, ashes of Ilion and you, ghosts of my companions, I take you as witnesses that in your disaster I never retreated, either before the blows of the enemy or any other danger, and had my fate decreed it, I was worthy to die with you."

The author was a warrior of antique valor with a simple and unshakable devotion to duty, and he came by these qualities naturally. Raimond-Emery-Philippe-Josephe de Montesquiou, Duke of Fezensac, was born in 1784 into a distinguished noble family with a long tradition of military service. He entered the army in 1807 and participated in all the major campaigns under the Empire. He continued his career under Louis XVIII, Charles X, and Louis-Philippe, and died in 1867 after having retired as a lieutenant general.

Fezensac had no intention of writing a history of the Russian campaign or indulging in weighty philosophizing about it; indeed he originally wrote down his experiences to satisfy the curiosity of his family and friends. The modest journal which follows is nevertheless one of the most lucid and moving accounts to be found in the vast literature on the Russian campaign. Fezensac writes chiefly of the events he witnessed, and no observer could have been more admirably placed. The first part of the narrative, which takes the reader to the Battle of Borodino, is essentially an introduction; during this period the author served as a staff officer and moved in the highest circles of command, in frequent contact with the Emperor and the glittering constellation of generals around him. After Borodino, Fezensac was chosen to command the Fourth Regiment of Infantry, and at this point the narrative becomes more detailed. The long retreat from Moscow is the main subject of the journal; during almost the entire period the Fourth Regiment fought in the rear guard under the indomitable Marshal Ney, of whom Fezensac speaks long and devotedly.

The *Journal de la campagne de Russie en 1812* appeared as a slim volume in 1849. Sainte-Beuve reviewed it the following year in his *Causeries du lundi* and was warm in his praise: "The reflections which this simple account engenders are of more than one kind. The impression that it leaves on the mind is ineffaceable. Reading it, one can get an exact picture of this disaster, from its origins to its last consequences, and much better than from reading more general and more extensive accounts."

Fezensac's narrative enjoyed some popularity in the France of Napoleon III, and in 1863 the author published his *Souvenirs militaires*, embracing his entire military career from 1807 to 1814. Perhaps interest in the history of the First Empire was linked to the fortunes of the Second. In any event, the publishing history of Fezensac's journals ended with Sedan.

In recent years both the scholar and the general reader have shown renewed interest in the 1812 campaign; that interest was whetted by the discovery, publication, and translation of Caulaincourt's journals in the 1930s, and more recently by a new English edition of Ségur's memoirs. And since Fezensac's little book has lost none of the charm that Sainte-Beuve found in it a century ago, it seems only right that it too should be available in translation to modern readers.

Introduction

The text of the journal has been reproduced in its entirety: the several charts and documents appended to the original edition have been included with one exception—a rather long list of all the officers of the Fourth Regiment. In translation every attempt has been made to preserve the simple but eloquent style of the French. Russian place names have been transliterated into their English equivalents, and several explanatory footnotes have been added by the editor and are so indicated.

LEE KENNETT

PREFACE

It is not a history of the campaign that I write. I am far from having such pretension. It is my personal journal; it is the faithful account of what happened before my eyes. Thus I will simply tell what I have seen and what has happened to me, while adding a word about the army's operations in general. The events of which I was witness are sufficiently remarkable that some day this writing may be read with some interest. At first it was only destined for my family and friends, but the favorable reception it has had now encourages me to publish it.

The two successive posts of aide-de-camp to the Prince of Neuchâtel and colonel of an infantry regiment which I held during this campaign divide the journal quite naturally into two parts: the first includes the conquest of Lithuania and of the Russian provinces until after the battle of the Moskva; the second embraces the occupation of Moscow and the retreat to the Oder. This second part will be longer than the first, since the Third Corps, of which my regiment was part, played a great role in the retreat, and since my new post as colonel of a regiment put me in a better position to see at close hand many interesting details.

PART ONE

CHAPTER ONE

The French and Russian armies

Declaration of war

Passage of the Niemen

Headquarters at Vilna

The two Russian corps

Conquest of all Lithuania

Headquarters at Glubokoye

Movements of the Russians

Combats before Vitebsk

Taking the town

Cantonments

SINCE THE CONCLUSION OF THE treaty of peace at Tilsit and its renewal at Erfurt, several causes of dissatisfaction had arisen between France and Russia. The Emperor Napoleon had seized the Hanseatic towns, and particularly Oldenburg, which belonged to the brother-in-law of Emperor Alexander; his troops occupied Prussia and all of Germany, and he insisted upon Russia's full and complete adherence to the Continental System. Emperor Alexander refused to persevere in a system which would have brought total ruin to the commerce of his empire, and for his part he demanded the evacuation of Prussia and the Hanseatic towns. War seemed inevitable; at the beginning of 1812 the two armies advanced, one to defend Russian territory, the other to invade it. Never on our side had such imposing masses been gathered: eleven corps of infantry, four corps of heavy cavalry, and the Imperial Guard formed a total of more than 500,000 men, protected by 1,200 cannon.[1] To form this prodigious army, recruiting was done in France, Italy, Germany, and Poland; Austria and Prussia had not dared to refuse their contingents. There were also troops from Illyria and Dalmatia, and even some battalions of Portuguese and Spaniards, astounded to find themselves at the other end of Europe and engaged in such an enterprise. Sweden maintained her neutrality; the peace concluded with Turkey now permitted the Russians to unite all their forces against this formidable invasion.

While the various corps of the Grand Army were rapidly crossing Germany, the Emperor Napoleon had stopped at Dresden and had summoned all the sovereigns of the Confederation of the Rhine, even the Emperor of Austria and the King of Prussia. He spent several days presiding over this assembly of kings, whom he seemed to find pleasure in humiliating by the splendor of his power.

I was at that time a squadron chief and aide-de-camp to the Duke of Feltre,[2] my father-in-law, who was Minister of War; I told him of my desire to make this campaign, and at his request the Prince of Neuchâtel,[3] Major General of the Grand Army, was good enough to take me into his service as aide-de-camp. At the beginning of May I reported to Posen, where headquarters were being established. I passed through Wesel, Magdeburg, and Berlin, which I found had been transformed into a stronghold. In order not to disrupt the march of the troops, and at the same time to preserve the dignity of the King of Prussia,

---

[1] The total number of the army at the time of the crossing of the Niemen was 414,000 men; but by adding the Ninth Corps and the Loison Division, which only entered the line later, and the numerous detachments which came continually to join the various corps, the administrators, the civil employees, and non-combatants, one easily arrives at the figure of 500,000 men who participated in all or a part of this campaign.

[2] Henri-Jacques-Guillaume Clarke, created Duke of Feltre in 1809, served as Napoleon's Minister of War from 1807 to 1814. Fezensac married Clarke's daughter in 1808. [Ed.]

[3] Louis-Alexandre Berthier, created Prince of Neuchâtel in 1806. [Ed.]

it had been decided that this prince would retire to Potsdam with his guard, while Berlin would be under the command of a French general. The capital, along with the rest of Prussia, was subjected to military billeting and requisitions of all kinds. The vexations to which the inhabitants of a country were subjected by the passage of our armies is well known, but never were they greater than at this period. It was not enough that the inhabitants feed their guests according to the custom established during our stay in Germany; we took their livestock as well; we requisitioned their horses and wagons, and kept them until we could find others to replace them. I often encountered peasants fifty leagues[4] from their villages, hauling the baggage of some regiment; and in the end these unfortunates were lucky if they could run off and abandon their horses.

At Posen I found all the officers attached to headquarters who had not accompanied the Emperor to Dresden, as well as several regiments of the Imperial Guard, troops belonging to various army corps, artillery trains, and materiel of all sorts. Never had such immense preparations been seen. The Emperor had collected all the forces of Europe for this expedition; and each, following his example, had brought along all that he might need. Each officer had at least one carriage, and the generals had several; servants and horses abounded.

Soon headquarters was moved to Thorn, and thence to Gumbinnen, by way of Osterode, Heilsberg, and Guttstadt—famous sites in the war of 1807. The Emperor rejoined us at Thorn and then went to visit Danzig and Koenigsberg before coming to Gumbinnen. It was in this town that the last hopes for peace were shattered. M. de Narbonne returned from Vilna, bringing Emperor Alex-

---

[4] The French *lieue* or league, frequently referred to in this journal, was approximately two and one-half miles. [Ed.]

ander's rejection of the propositions that had been made to him. At his final audience, the Emperor told him that he had decided upon war, that he would wage it steadfastly, and that even if we should be the masters of Moscow, he would still not think his cause lost. "To be sure, Sire," replied M. de Narbonne, "you will still be the most powerful monarch in Asia." The declaration of war followed shortly after this final gesture: the two Emperors announced it in proclamations whose style varied greatly. Napoleon proclaimed it in a prophetic tone: "Russia is being impelled by fate; her destiny must be accomplished." Alexander said to his army: "I am with you: God is against the aggressor."

From Gumbinnen the army entered Poland to attain the Niemen. When we crossed the frontier we were struck by the surprising contrast which the two countries presented, and by the rapid change in the ways of the inhabitants. Everything in Prussia bespeaks prosperity and civilization; the houses are well built, the fields cultivated. As soon as one enters Poland one encounters only the image of servitude and misery, brutish peasants, a detestable class of Jews, fields that are scarcely tilled, and for houses, miserable huts that are quite as filthy as their inhabitants.

The Russian army gathered on the banks of the Niemen at this time was divided into two parts: the first, commanded directly by General Barclay de Tolly, the general-in-chief, protected the crossings near Kovno; the second, commanded by Prince Bagration, defended Grodno. Together they formed a total of 230,000 men; on the extreme left, 68,000 men commanded by General Tormasov covered Volhynia; on the extreme right, 34,000 men defended Courland. Russia thus had 330,000 men under arms, and France about 400,000.

In this state of affairs the Emperor Napoleon's plan

was promptly made. He decided to force the passage of the Niemen near Kovno and march rapidly into Lithuania, in order to separate General Barclay from General Bagration. After he had directed the Tenth Corps toward Tilsit for an attack on Courland and placed the Fifth, Seventh, and Eighth Corps at Novogrodeck, opposite Prince Bagration, he himself moved toward the Niemen with the Imperial Guard, the First, Second, Third, and Fourth Corps, and the first two cavalry corps. The banks of the Niemen were reconnoitered; the place for crossing was chosen a little above Kovno. The army gathered there on the evening of the twenty-third of June, and three bridges were built in very short order.

Day had scarcely dawned before the First Corps was across. The Second and Third and the cavalry reserve followed. The Emperor's tents were pitched on a height which dominated the opposite shore. There we gathered to watch this magnificent spectacle. General Barclay, who had only one division at this spot, could not contest our crossing. We took Kovno without resistance, and the Emperor took his headquarters there. From there the different army corps marched on Vilna. General Barclay withdrew at their approach. Several times I was sent on mission to the generals who commanded our troops, and I had many occasions to admire the bearing of the regiments, their enthusiasm, and the regularity and order in their movements. The Emperor rejoined the advance guard on the evening of the 27th, and the next morning, after light resistance, our troops entered Vilna, where they were received with acclamations.

The campaign had begun but five days before, and already the Emperor's plan had succeeded. The two Russian armies were separated: General Barclay made his retreat toward the entrenched camp at Drissa, on the Dvina, thus uncovering Lithuania in order to protect the road to

Saint Petersburg; General Bagration had abandoned the banks of the Niemen to try to rejoin him, but our troops were already between them. During the Emperor's stay at Vilna, the corps of the Grand Army spread throughout Lithuania in pursuit of the two Russian armies. The King of Naples,[5] with the cavalry and the Second and Third Corps, followed the retrograde movement of General Barclay toward Drissa. The First Corps, on the road to Minsk, cut the communications of Prince Bagration, who was being closely pressed by the Fifth, Seventh, and Eighth.[6] The Fourth and Sixth Corps remained in the vicinity of Vilna, while the Imperial Guard formed its garrison. Each day was marked by a success; each officer who was dispatched brought back good news. Yet the season was not favorable to us; a suffocating heat was succeeded by rain which fell in torrents. This sudden change in temperature, added to the difficulty in obtaining forage, caused a high mortality among the army's horses; the bad weather completed the destruction of the roads, which often were nothing more than long planks thrown down across marshes. We were already feeling the shortage of food. The army was living on the resources of the countryside, and these resources, inconsiderable in themselves, were even less so before the harvest; already soldiers were turning to indiscipline and pillage,[7] but all seemed justified by success.

During this time the Emperor gave thought to profiting from the important conquest which he had so fortunately made during the first days of the campaign.

---

5 Joachim Murat, King of Naples from 1808 to 1815. [Ed.]

6 These last three corps, placed under the command of Prince Jerome, King of Westphalia, thus formed the extreme right of the army.

7 I do not speak of the regiments, but of the stragglers marching by themselves, whose number was already great at this time.

The geographic position of Vilna first drew his attention. The Vilia River, which passes through it, is navigable to the Niemen, as is the Niemen to the sea. This consideration led the Emperor to make Vilna his principal depot. Stores gathered at Danzig and Koenigsberg were transported there and various fortifications were raised to protect the town from sudden attack. At the same time Napoleon neglected nothing in order to draw profit from the political importance of the capital of Lithuania. Hardly were we masters of Vilna before the Lithuanian nobility requested of him the re-establishment of the Kingdom of Poland. A diet assembled at Warsaw by his permission proclaimed this re-establishment and sent a deputation to Vilna to ask for the adherence of Lithuania and to solicit the protection of the Emperor. In a rather ambiguous reply Napoleon gave them to understand that he would decide after the event, declaring, however, that he had guaranteed to the Emperor of Austria the integrity of his territory, and that consequently they must renounce Galicia. This evasive response, far from discouraging the Poles, only spurred their zeal: they succumbed completely to the hope of recovering their independence. The deliberations of the Grand Duchy of Warsaw, providing for the re-establishment of the Kingdom of Poland, were formally accepted by Lithuania. This ceremony took place in the cathedral at Vilna, where all the nobility was assembled. Men could be seen there dressed in the ancient Polish costume, and women wearing ribbons in the red and violet of the national colors. After a solemn mass, the act of adherence was read and accepted by acclamation; they sang the *Te Deum*, and immediately after the ceremony the act of adherence was taken to the Duke of Bassano[8] for presentation to the Emperor, who received

---

8 Hugues-Bernard Maret, created Duke of Bassano in 1809. [Ed.]

it with favor. Immediately a civil government of Lithuania was organized, and its first measure was to order large levies of men. Amid these preparations the assemblies, balls, and concerts continued without interruption. Present at these celebrations, we could hardly recognize the capital of a country ravaged by two enemy armies, and whose inhabitants were reduced to misery and despair; and if the Lithuanians themselves seemed sometimes to remember this, it was in order to say that no sacrifice was too great for Poles when it came to the reestablishment of their country.[9]

The Emperor's stay in Vilna gave us an opportunity to observe the composition of the general staff in all its details. The Emperor had with him the Grand Marshal, the Grand Equerry, his aides-de-camp, his administrative officers, the aides-de-camp of his aides-de-camp, and several secretaries for his paper work. The Major General had eight or ten aides-de-camp, and the number of bureaux necessary for the work demanded in such a large army. The general staff, composed of a great number of officers of all ranks, was commanded by General Monthion. The administration, directed by Count Dumas, Intendant General, was sub-divided into the administrative services themselves (*ordonnateurs,* review inspectors, and *commissaires des guerres*), the medical service (physicians, surgeons, and pharmacists), the supply service in its different branches, and workers of all kinds. When the Prince of Neuchâtel reviewed them at Vilna, at a distance they looked like an army deployed for battle; but through a hapless fate, in spite of the zeal and the talents of the Intendant General, this immense administration was ineffectual from the beginning of the expedi-

---

[9] The disorder was so far advanced that the Sub-Perfect of Nevtroki (near Vilna) was robbed by the soldiers and arrived nearly naked in the village he was to administer.

tion, and became harmful in the end. Consider the gathering in one place of all which made up this staff; imagine the prodigious number of servants, of riding horses, of baggage of all sorts which followed it, and the reader will have some idea of the spectacle which headquarters presented. When the army moved, the Emperor took with him only a small number of officers, and all the rest departed in advance or followed in the rear. If they camped, there were tents only for the Emperor and the Prince of Neuchâtel; the generals and other officers bivouacked with the rest of the army.

The services which we performed as aides-de-camp to the Major General were not arduous. Every day two of us had duty, one to carry orders, and the other to receive dispatches and messengers. Thus our turn came every four or five days, unless one of us were sent as courier; this happened rarely, for staff officers were usually sent. The Prince of Neuchâtel in his personal contacts with us displayed that mixture of kindness and brusqueness of which his character was composed. Often he seemed to ignore us completely, but when the occasion arose, we could be sure of his entire attention; moreover, during the course of his long military career, he had never failed to take an interest in the advancement of any officers who served under him. His billet was always the best house in the town after that of the Emperor, and since he personally stayed in the latter place, his quarters belonged to his aides-de-camp. One of them, M. Pernet, was charged with the details of the household, whose administration could have served as a model. The Prince of Neuchâtel himself, in the midst of all his preoccupations, did not forget us; he desired that his aides-de-camp lack for nothing, and he was good enough to make inquiries in this regard very frequently. In the midst of war it was very satisfying not to have to worry about such things, and to find oneself

Part One, Chapter One

better fed and better lodged than the rest of the army without the slightest effort. The composition of the headquarters staff also made it an agreeable place. Among the officers attached to the Emperor or to the generals of his household were MM. Fernand de Chabot, Eugene d'Astorg, de Castellane, de Mortemart, and de Talmont. The aides-de-camp of the Prince of Neuchâtel were MM. de Girardin, de Flahaut, Alfred de Noailles, Anatole de Montesquiou, Lecouteulx, Adrien d'Astorg, and myself. In such a gathering one could almost think himself still in France.

We saw little of the Prince of Neuchâtel, since we had no work with him. He spent almost all of the day in his bureau sending orders conformable to the Emperor's instructions. Never was there greater exactitude, more complete subservience, or more absolute devotion. It was while writing at night that he had to recover from the fatigue of the day. Often he was called in the middle of his sleep to change all the work of the preceding day, and sometimes his only rewards were reprimands that were undeserved, or at least extremely severe. But his zeal never flagged; no physical fatigue, no paper work was beyond his strength; nothing could destroy his patience. In short, if the Prince of Neuchâtel's position never gave him the occasion to develop the talents necessary to command great armies himself, it would be impossible to find anyone who possessed to a higher degree the physical and mental qualities suitable for the functions which he fulfilled under a person such as the Emperor.

In the first days of July Napoleon decided to move his headquarters forward in order to follow the movement of the army. Glubokoye, a small town thirty leagues from Vilna in the direction of Vitebsk, seemed to him to be the most suitable central point. From there he could march

Headquarters at Glubokoye

with equal facility on the camp at Drissa to his left, or Minsk to his right, or straight ahead to the area where the two Russian armies might still attempt a juncture.

The Fourth and Sixth Corps and the Imperial Guard left Vilna successively to take this latter direction. The Emperor, intending to make the movement very rapidly, sent almost all of the staff officers ahead.

The aides-de-camp of the Prince of Neuchâtel left Vilna on July 12, and in five days' march we arrived at Glubokoye.[10] The countryside which we crossed was generally attractive and well cultivated, the villages miserable as those in Poland and plundered by our troops. We encountered several regiments of the Young Guard; among others, I noticed a regiment of flankers, composed of very young men. This regiment had come from Saint-Denis and had had no rest save a day at Mayence and a day at Marienwerder on the Vistula; after their arrival the soldiers were still being drilled on days of march, because the Emperor had not found them sufficiently trained. Consequently, this regiment was the first destroyed: already the soldiers were collapsing from fatigue along the roads.

Glubokoye, a small town built of wood, was only inhabited by some Jews; the forests and lakes which surrounded it gave it a somber and wild aspect, and our memories of Vilna did not help make our stay an agreeable one. The Emperor arrived there on the 18th, when the enemy's plans led him to adopt new measures.

Prince Bagration, by the rapidity of his march, had eluded the pursuit of the Fifth and Eighth Corps, and was beyond their reach. The Emperor, very angry, blamed the King of Westphalia[11] and put the entire right wing

---

10 By way of Lavarishki, Mikhalevichi, Cheki, and Danielovich.

11 Jerome Bonaparte, Napoleon's younger brother, had been made King of Westphalia in 1807. [Ed.]

under the orders of the Prince of Eckmühl.[12] The King, very angry himself, left the army. But inevitably these new arrangements made us lose time. Prince Bagration took advantage of this: on the 17th he crossed the Beresina at Bobruysk and marched on Moghilev to rejoin General Barclay at Vitebsk. All that the Prince of Eckmühl could do was to reach Moghilev first and try to bar his path. General Barclay, informed of these events, and seeing that it was impossible for Prince Bagration to reach the camp at Drissa, decided to move to meet him before Vitebsk. This fortified camp, which had been built with such great effort, was abandoned precipitately on the 18th,[13] and the Russian army moved in all haste toward Vitebsk. General Wittgenstein remained before Polotsk, on the right bank of the Dvina, in order to defend the road to Saint Petersburg. The Second and Sixth Corps moved toward Polotsk to oppose him. The Third and Fourth Corps, the cavalry and the Guard rapidly pursued the large Russian army towards Vitebsk. Headquarters left Glubokoye the 22nd and arrived at Beshenkovichi on the 24th. All indications led us to believe that the enemy would offer battle before Vitebsk. The enthusiasm in the regiments ran very high, and we all shared it.

On the morning of the 25th the Prince of Neuchâtel ordered me to cross the army's right to Moghilev, where I was to find the Prince of Eckmühl; my instructions directed me to send word to the Emperor immediately of anything new which I might learn. A Polish officer accompanied me in order to question the inhabitants. The

---

12 Louis-Nicolas Davout, created Prince of Eckmühl in 1809. [Ed.]

13 The fortified camp at Drissa was the fantasy of General Phull, one of Alexander's military advisors. Had the Russian army chosen to stand there, the camp would undoubtedly have become its tomb. [Ed.]

Movements of the Russians

Emperor wanted to know most particularly the Prince of Eckmühl's position vis-à-vis Prince Bagration, and if the Fifth and Eighth Corps were at last able to aid him. I left during the first cannon shots which announced the attack by the King of Naples.

Moghilev is about thirty-five leagues from Babinovichi. At Sienno we took the post road, but since all the horses had been carried off, we were hard put to continue our trip. My companion was a great help, taking me to Polish chateaux whose lords furnished us with horses. The countryside was quiet, and there was no news. Night found us at Koshanov. General Grouchy commanded a corps of cavalry here, with an advance guard at Orsha under General Colbert. Before him was a Russian corps which blocked the road to Smolensk. In the early morning of the 26th we arrived at Shklov, a very prosperous little town, and later in the morning at Moghilev, where the First Corps was located; I had a good opportunity to observe in this last town the order and discipline which always distinguished the troops of the Prince of Eckmühl. I learned from him that Prince Bagration had ascended the Dnieper from Stary-Bykhov and had attacked him without success on the 22nd and the 23rd. Renouncing his attempt to force a crossing at Moghilev, Prince Bagration had crossed the Dnieper at Stary-Bykhov and had retired in the direction of Smolensk. As for the Fifth and Eighth Corps, they were expected at Moghilev, and as soon as they arrived, the Prince of Eckmühl intended to ascend the Dnieper to Orsha in order to draw closer to the other corps. Thus Prince Bagration had eluded the efforts to surround him, but at the same time his juncture with General Barclay under the walls of Vitebsk was now impossible.

The 26th was a Sunday. The Prince of Eckmühl, upon

Part One, Chapter One

leaving the mass, received the Archimandrite and called upon him to recognize Emperor Napoleon as his sovereign, and to substitute his name for that of Emperor Alexander in the public prayers. In this connection he reminded him of the words of the Bible, "Render unto Caesar that which is Caesar's," adding that Caesar referred to him who was the strongest. The Archimandrite promised to comform to these instructions, but he did so in a tone that showed how little he approved.

I left that evening by the same road; the next day, as I was approaching the army, I learned that the three days of my absence had been filled with three brilliant engagements, in which Ostrovno had been seized and the Russian army driven from one position after another up to the walls of Vitebsk. I crossed the battlefields which were still covered with the debris of these three battles and arrived at headquarters on the evening of the 26th, where I made my report to the Emperor and the Prince of Neuchâtel.

The army was camped in order of battle opposite the Russian army, separated from it by a stream called the Luchosa; the Emperor's tents were pitched on a height near the center. I spent the evening recounting my mission and listening in turn to an account of the engagements that had just been fought. I was pleased to hear that several aides-de-camp of the Prince Neuchâtel had distinguished themselves, and that the fine conduct of the troops promised even greater successes when the occasion presented itself. We were expecting a general engagement the next morning: great was our surprise when we saw at daybreak that the enemy had withdrawn. General Barclay had, in fact, received word that Prince Bagration, unable to seize the bridge at Moghilev, had crossed the Dnieper below this town and headed for Smolensk, the only place where he might effect a juncture; and General

Taking the town

Barclay, not wanting to offer battle before this juncture, had decided to leave Vitebsk and march toward Smolensk.[14]

The Emperor entered Vitebsk and sent troops in pursuit of the enemy. After two days, when the retreat toward Smolensk was apparent, he decided to give the army some repose; favorable news from the detached corps encouraged him further in this resolve. On the left the Tenth Corps had conquered Courland and was approaching Riga. The Duke of Reggio,[15] at the head of the Second and Sixth Corps, had just beaten General Wittgenstein before Polotsk, while on the right the Seventh Corps and the Austrians were progressing against General Tormasov between the Bug and the Narev. The Corps of the Grand Army were cantonned between the Dnieper and the Dvina; the Fifth Corps, on the right at Moghilev, and then in succession the Eighth, First, Third, and Fourth, whose left was at Vely, above Vitebsk. The cavalry had the advance guard, and the Imperial Guard and headquarters were at Vitebsk.

---

14 The engagements at Ostrovno and Vitebsk were fought by the cavalry of the King of Naples and the Fourth Corps. In one of these engagements two companies of *voltigeurs* of the Ninth Regiment (Fourth Corps) had advanced very far into the plain, and were charged by the entire Russian cavalry. The two companies in serried ranks repulsed this attack and rejoined the French army, which, united on the surrounding heights, had watched this fine action and encouraged the soldiers by its cheers.

15 Nicolas-Charles Oudinot, created Duke of Reggio in 1809. [Ed.]

CHAPTER TWO

Stay at Vitebsk
Situation of the army
March on Smolensk
Taking the city
Affair at Valutino
The Emperor's Plans
March on Moscow
Battle of the Moscowa

THE TOWN OF VITEBSK, THE ONLY sizeable one which we had encountered since Vilna, offered a pleasant sojourn for headquarters. Napoleon used the time to complete the organization of the provisional government of Lithuania, which he had established at Vilna. Since it was to our interest to spare Vitebsk, and since we had entered it unopposed, the town was not looted. Vitebsk, the capital of White Russia, is situated on the Dvina at an equal distance from Saint Petersburg and Moscow, and is a well-populated commercial center. The province, which has been united to Russia for a long time, has acquired Russian habits and customs: thus at Vitebsk we found none of the enthusiasm of Vilna. The inhabitants received us more as conquerors than liberators. But the political interest of the Emperor was to extend the frontiers of Poland as far as possible, and the province of Vitebsk was declared an integral part of this kingdom. It received a governor and an intendant who were given orders to treat it as an ally rather than a subject territory.

A new sort of disorder called for Napoleon's attention at this time. The peasants of the region, hearing talk of liberty and independence, took it upon themselves to rise up against their lords and indulge themselves in a chaotic license. The nobility of Vitebsk complained to the Emperor, who ordered severe measures to re-establish order.

As for us, since we had nothing to do with administration or the maintenance of order, we spent our time talking about our past exploits and promising ourselves new ones. Never had a campaign begun so brilliantly. All of Lithuania had been conquered in a month, and almost without fighting; the army, gathered on the banks of the Dnieper and the Dvina, only awaited the order of its leader to penetrate into the interior of Russia. Moreover, the enemy's movements since the crossing of the Niemen led us to believe that he had no fixed plan. At first they had sought to defend the Niemen with Vilna as their strongpoint, then they had hastily abandoned this river, destroyed the stores at Vilna, let communications between their armies be cut, and had exposed all of Lithuania. We had seen General Barclay retire on the Dvina to the camp at Drissa to await Prince Bagration, who, since the French army had crossed the Niemen, could not possibly join him there; then, abandoning without a fight this fortified camp upon which so much effort had been lavished, he had stopped for a few days before Vitebsk, only to leave it to rejoin Prince Bagration under the walls of Smolensk. The superiority of the Emperor's maneuvers was incontestable; the talents of our generals and the bravery of our troops were beyond question. If there were a battle, we could expect victory. If the enemy avoided one, we would organize Lithuania, take Riga, and next year we would begin the campaign with immense advantages. The Emperor shared these bright expectations. In a conversation which he had at Vitebsk with M. de Narbonne, he estimated 130,000 men to be in the two Russian armies before

Smolensk. He planned to have 170,000 with the Guard, the cavalry and the First, Third, Fourth, Fifth, and Eighth Corps; if they avoided a battle, he would not go beyond Smolensk; if he won a complete victory, perhaps he would march straight to Moscow; but in any case a battle, even indecisive, seemed to him a long step toward peace.

Nevertheless, those of reflective temperament and the experienced officers were not without some concern. They had seen the army dwindle by a third since the passage of the Niemen with scarcely any fighting, simply through the impossibility of providing for its subsistence in any regular fashion, and through the difficulty in obtaining anything, even by pillage, from a countryside which was poor to begin with and which had already been ravaged by the Russian army. They noticed the frightful mortality among the horses, the dismounting of a part of the cavalry, the difficulty in hauling the artillery, and the abandonment of ambulances and medical vehicles; thus, when they went into the hospitals, they found the sick being given little treatment. They asked themselves not only what might happen to this army if it were beaten, but also how it could withstand the losses which would result from further marches and more serious fighting. Amid these causes for concern they were struck by the admirable order with which the Russian army had conducted its retreat, always screened by numbers of Cossacks, never abandoning a single cannon, a single wagon, a single casualty. They knew, moreover, that Emperor Alexander had called all Russians to the defense of their homeland, and that each step which we took into the interior of the country would diminish our forces and increase those of our enemy.

The Emperor spent fifteen days at Vitebsk; every morning at six o'clock he witnessed the parade of the Guard in front of his palace; he insisted that everyone attend, and even went so far as to have several buildings pulled down in order to enlarge the parade ground. There, in the presence of the staff and the Guard, he took up in the greatest detail all the aspects of military administration; the *commissaires des guerres* and the medical officers were called upon to report on the state of the supply system, how the patients were being cared for in the hospitals, how many bandages had been collected for the wounded. Often they received very harsh reprimands or criticism. No one showed more concern for the subsistence and the hospitals of the army than did Napoleon. But it is not enough to give orders: the orders must be capable of execution. With the rapidity of our movements, the concentration of troops in one location, the wretched state of the roads and the difficulty of nourishing horses, how could they possibly make regular distributions or organize the hospital service satisfactorily? The soldiers, who knew nothing of these impossibilities, found fault with the dedication and sometimes the honesty of the administrators; they lamented, as they died miserably along the roads or in the ambulances: "It's a shame, for the Emperor is trying to take care of us."

It was at one of these parades that General Friant was installed as commander of the Foot Grenadiers of the Guard, in place of General Dorsenne, who had died in Spain. Napoleon himself received him at the head of the Grenadiers of the Guard, sword in hand, and embraced him.

Meanwhile, in the first days of August, the Russians assaulted some of our advance posts with indifferent success. Requisite measures were taken and the order was given to draw rations for fifteen days, the Emperor having decided to march on Smolensk by the left bank of the Dnieper. This movement began on the 10th and all of the army corps took the highway from Orsha to Smolensk. A pontoon bridge was built at Rasasno; the Third and Fourth Corps, the cavalry and the Imperial Guard crossed it and moved rapidly along the road to Smolensk, while the First and Eighth Corps, already at Dubrovno and Orsha, marched in the same direction; the Fifth Corps crossed the Dnieper at Moghilev and supported the movement on the right. All of these movements were executed with a rapidity and a precision to which the Russians have paid tribute. The Emperor left Vitebsk on the 13th and crossed the Dnieper at Rasasno. As early as the 14th the enemy's advance guard at Krasnii was driven back by the King of Naples and Marshal Ney.

On the 15th headquarters was at Korytnia, and the advance guard was approaching Smolensk. The Emperor, very occupied with military operations, did not wish to receive any good wishes for his birthday. He spent the evening questioning Russian prisoners in great detail, and their accounts, along with the rapid movements of the Russian army, led him to believe that Smolensk was being evacuated.

At dawn on the 16th some officers from headquarters and a number of servants who had gone forward to locate billets found the advance guard engaged with the enemy, and we soon learned that the news of the evacuation of the town was false. General Barclay, who was covering Smolensk from the other side of the river, followed us hastily as soon as he perceived the general movement of our army along the left bank; he ordered Prince Bagration to occupy Dorogobuzh in the rear, on the road to Moscow, to cover his communications with that capital, while he himself prepared to defend Smolensk.

The Emperor ordered his troops forward, and as the enemy rear guard retired before us, we arrived that evening before the walls of Smolensk.

Smolensk was famous in the ancient wars between

March on Smolensk

Russia and Poland, who fought over the city for a long time; but Poland having ceded it to Russia a half century ago, it has become completely Russian. Its high walls with their towers still attest to its former importance. The fortifications were far from being built on the modern system, or offering for regular defense the advantage of our fortresses; but the great extent of its walls over an area of nearly 4,000 *toises*,[1] their height of twenty-five feet and their thickness of ten, the wide moat and covered way which defended their approaches, all made a spirited attack very difficult; the ramparts were well furnished with artillery, the suburbs in front of the walls were fortified, and firing slits had been cut in the houses. On the other side of the Dnieper there was a suburb shaped in the form of an amphitheater; the Russian army was in position on the heights which dominate this suburb, ready if need be to come to the aid of the divisions which were to defend Smolensk.

In the evening the Emperor reconnoitered all the area around the town. He placed his army in a half circle with the wings resting on the Dnieper; the Third Corps on the extreme left, then successively the First and Fifth Corps; finally the cavalry under the King of Naples on the extreme right; the Imperial Guard in reserve behind the center with headquarters. The Fourth Corps remained in the rear; the Eighth, which had made a wrong movement, was not present.

We spent the night in bivouac, and in spite of our expectations, the next morning all was calm. I learned later that the Emperor thought he would be attacked by the Russians before the walls, and he preferred to await them. But by two o'clock, seeing that nothing was going to happen, he ordered the attack. The troops of the Third and

---

1 The *toise* was slightly over three feet. [Ed.]

Part One, Chapter Two

First Corps carried the suburbs; the Russians, driven from the covered way, retreated into the city, and our breaching batteries opened fire. But the walls were so thick that the cannon had little effect. I had occasion to see this for myself, since the Emperor ordered me to visit the batteries. Following the unanimous advice of the artillery officers, he abandoned the idea of mounting the assault that evening. He ordered the firing stopped and put off the taking of the town until the following day.

As we returned to the tents we talked of the events of the day; the former officers of the Army of Egypt remarked that the thickness of the walls at Smolensk reminded them of those of Saint-Jean d'Acre.

At dawn of the 18th some soldiers noticed that the ramparts were no longer manned; they entered the town and discovered that it had been abandoned. We took possession immediately. The Russians had set fire to it during the night as they were leaving; the bridges were destroyed and the Russian army ranged in battle on the right bank. A very lively fusillade broke out between the two banks, and continued all day while we labored on the bridges. That evening and into the night General Barclay continued his retreat along the road to Moscow, after having set fire to the suburbs on the right bank. We established headquarters at Smolensk.

On the 19th the Third Corps, followed by the First, crossed the Dnieper and pursued the enemy; Marshal Ney caught up with them near Valutino Hill and beat them soundly after a lively resistance. The Eighth Corps had been ordered to cross the Dnieper above Smolensk and strike the enemy on the flank; this corps had not yet arrived, and its absence kept us from completing the day's victory. I do not know what caused it to delay its march or change its direction. Whatever the cause, the Emperor

Affair at Valutino

was very bitter at the Duke of Abrantès over it, and refused to see him the first time he presented himself.[2]

The Third Corps performed so brilliantly on that day that the Russians thought they had engaged the Imperial Guard; the Emperor, who had been present at the encounter, went back to the battlefield the next day; there, amidst the dead, he reviewed the troops which had fought on the previous day. After expressing his satisfaction, and his regret at the loss of General Gudin, who fell at the head of his division, he accorded the regiment many honors and promotions. The 127th, which had been recently formed, received an eagle.[3]

The advance guard continued the pursuit of the enemy while the Emperor returned to Smolensk to consider new plans.

Our losses in the engagement at Smolensk and Valutino amounted to more than 8,000 men; the enemy's losses were greater, no doubt, but these were still not the complete victories that could bring peace. We did not take a single prisoner; the Russian army continued to retire in the best order, always taking up another position further to the rear. Many of us thought that the Emperor was going to halt and place his army again between the Dvina and the Dnieper, with even more advantage now that the taking of Smolensk made us masters of both banks of the Dnieper. The Tenth Corps could still take Riga before the end of the campaign, and by spending the winter in this position the army could repair its losses, the govern-

---

[2] Jean-Andoche Junot, created Duke of Abrantès in 1808. Junot never recovered from this disgrace; he committed suicide in 1813. [Ed.]

[3] Napoleon gave these eagles to the French regiments in 1804 to surmount the regimental standards. Since they symbolized the Emperor's presence they were always objects of veneration. [Ed.]

ment of Lithuania could be completed, and the province could furnish troops, upon whose loyalty we could rely. This plan would perhaps have been the wisest, but the Emperor, accustomed to dominating events, could not accept it. He wanted a battle, and he thought that by pushing the Russians smartly along the road to Moscow he would force them sooner or later to offer this decisive battle so long desired, and whose consequence should be peace. But if we marched on we would have to resign ourselves to sacrifices; we should expect to see the villages burned, the inhabitants dispersed, the crops, livestock, and forage carried off or destroyed. The manner in which the Russians had treated Smolensk showed that no sacrifice on their part was too great if it harmed us or hindered our operations. The King of Naples, who was still with the advance guard, insisted repeatedly that the troops were worn out, and that the horses, which were eating nothing but roof straw, could not withstand the fatigue; we would risk losing all if we went any farther. His opinion did not prevail, and the order was given to continue the march.

The headquarters staff had several days of rest in Smolensk, if indeed one could call a stay in such a town repose. When we entered it we found fires in several places, the Russian wounded agonizing in the flames, and the inhabitants fleeing their houses. At length we put out the fires, and the houses which had survived the holocaust were given over to pillage. In the midst of this disorder the inhabitants vanished. But when we entered the cathedral church we found them huddled there, dressed in rags and dying from hunger. The Emperor was extremely angry at these excesses. One evening he had the drums beat the long roll to assemble the Guard, which was garrisoned there; he assigned a district to each regiment and gave strict orders to stop the pillage.

Before his departure he took care of the administration of his new conquests; he named a governor and an intendant for the province of Smolensk, and he organized a large supply depot, food stores, and a hospital.

The army marched in three columns: the King of Naples commanded the advance guard; the First, Third, and Eighth Corps, the Imperial Guard and the headquarters staff followed along the highway. The Fifth Corps formed the right column, and the Fourth that on the left; each was one or two leagues from the highway.

The road from Smolensk to Moscow crosses vast plains interrupted by several hills. There are also forests in the vicinity of Dorogobuzh and Vyazma. The country is heavily populated, and the fields are well cultivated, the villages are built of wood as in the rest of Russia. The larger towns are distinctive in their stone houses and numerous steeples; sometimes one encounters magnificent chateaux, especially near Moscow. It is easy to tell, without consulting a map, that one has left Poland. The Jews have disappeared, and the Russian peasants, although as far removed from liberty and civilization as the Polish ones, resemble them not at all. The Russians are large and strong, while the Poles are puny and weak; the Poles are brutish, while the Russians are only wild. In ordinary warfare this countryside might offer some subsistence; but at this time the Russian army, adhering to its system, burned the houses and destroyed everything along the way; as we followed, we completed the ravaging of what little remained. It was impossible to attack the enemy infantry; the advance guard could only engage their light cavalry, which simply defended itself long enough to permit the rest of the army to retire unmolested. The activity of the King of Naples exceeded all praise, as did his bravery. Never did he leave the forefront of the advance guard;

there he directed in person the fire of his riflemen and exposed himself to the fire of the enemy, for whom his hat with its white plumes served as a target.

The Emperor, believing that each day would see the enemy turn and offer battle, was thus drawn down the road to Moscow, disregarding the fatigue of his troops, and without reflecting that already he was out of communication with the other army corps.

Headquarters was at Dorogobuzh on the 25th, at Stavkavoz on the 26th and the 27th, near Semlevo on the 28th, and a league from Vyazma on the 29th. On the 30th we were at Vyazma, the 31st at Velishchevo, and the 1st of September at Gzhatsk, some thirty-eight leagues from Moscow. We were particularly saddened at the little town of Vyazma, whose houses were engulfed by flames. As the Emperor was passing through it he spied some soldiers who were busy pillaging a dram shop which had begun to burn. This spectacle sent him into a rage; he rushed upon them with curses and blows from his riding crop. The impossibility of assailing the Russian army, and the ravages it had committed in our path disrupted his plans, and gave him that temper to which those around him often fell victim. At last he learned at Gzhatsk that the Russian army had turned to offer him battle; never was news more welcome.

General Kutusov had succeeded General Barclay in the command of the Russian army; Emperor Alexander placed all his hopes in this new general, and his confidence was shared by the army and the nation. In order to merit this regard, Kutusov resolved to fight a major battle; indeed the proximity to Moscow made this step necessary. Emperor Alexander had gone to this town in July. His presence there had generated the liveliest enthusiasm; the assembled nobility and merchants had unanimously voted immense levies of men and money. They had been given the positive assurance that the enemy would never enter

Moscow. Thus everything committed the Russian general to trying the test of battle before delivering up the city. Kutusov chose the position at Borodino, behind the stream called the Koloch and some five leagues in front of Mozhaisk and twenty-five leagues from Moscow. When the Emperor was informed of this, he notified his generals, and spent three days at Gzhatsk making his plans. The army marched again on the 4th and drove in the enemy's advance guard. On the morning of the 5th, we stood facing our opponents.

General Kutusov had arranged in the order of battle 100,000 infantry and 30,000 horse, comprising the two Russian armies, augmented by reinforcements recently arrived and the Moscow militia.

The Koloch covered his right which rested upon the Moskva River and was defended by numerous batteries; the center was placed behind a ravine and protected by three strong redoubts; the left was in front of the wood which is crossed by the old road to Moscow, and was likewise fortified by a redoubt. Another redoubt, built some 1,200 *toises* in front of the center, served as a sort of advance guard for this position. The Emperor ordered its capture. On the morning of the 5th, General Compans of the First Corps carried it, and finally held it after it had been taken and retaken three times. Our army then approached and camped opposite the enemy. The Emperor had his tents pitched on a hill near the road behind the village of Valuyevo. The Imperial Guard camped about him in a square.

The day of the 6th was spent in reconnoitering the enemy's position and in placing the troops in order of battle. The Emperor resolved to attack the Russian center and left, taking the redoubts built at those points. In consequence, he placed the Fifth Corps on the right on the old highway; the First and Third Corps in the center opposite the large redoubts; the cavalry behind them near the redoubt taken the day before; the Imperial Guard in reserve; the Fourth Corps on the extreme left near the village of Borodino. The total of those present did not exceed 120,000. It is said that some suggested to the Emperor to maneuver on his right in order to turn the enemy's left and force him to abandon his position, but he wanted the battle; he had long believed it necessary, and he feared to let the chance pass.

We spent this entire day at headquarters, and the impression that it made is still clear in my memory. There was something somber and imposing in the sight of these two armies which were preparing to slaughter each other. All the regiments had received the order to put on parade uniforms, as if for a holiday; the Imperial Guard, in particular, seemed to be waiting for a procession rather than a battle. Nothing is more striking than the sangfroid of these old soldiers; on their faces were neither anxiety nor exhilaration. A new battle was to them but one victory more, and to share this noble confidence one had only to look at them.

In the evening M. de Beausset, the Prefect of the Palace, arrived from Paris and presented to the Emperor a large portrait of his son; this event seemed a favorable sign. Colonel Fabvier arrived soon afterward; he came from Spain and brought the Emperor news of the state of our affairs after the loss of the battle of Salamanca. Napoleon, despite his deep preoccupation, conversed with him all evening.

On the 7th, at two o'clock in the morning, the two armies stood under arms; each awaited with anxiety the outcome of this terrible day. Each side had to conquer or perish; for us, a defeat would doom us irrevocably; for them, it would mean the loss of Moscow and the destruction of a great army, Russia's only hope. Thus, on both sides great pains were taken to rouse the ardor of the soldiers. Each general spoke to his men in the language suitable to their ideas, their manners, and their customs. In the Russian army priests carrying a sacred image passed through the ranks: the kneeling soldiers received their benedictions, their exhortations, and their good wishes; General Kutusov reminded the soldiers of the religious conviction which they all possessed. "It is in this faith," he said, "that I wish to fight and win. It is in this faith that I wish to conquer or die, and may my dying eyes behold our victory. Soldiers, think of your wives and children who call for your protection; think of your Emperor who is watching you, and before tomorrow's sun has disappeared, you will have inscribed your faith and your loyalty in the fields of your fatherland, with the blood of the aggressor and his legions." In the French army the marshals gathered around the Emperor near the redoubt to receive his final orders. At the first rays of dawn he cried: "Behold the sun of Austerlitz!" The drums were beaten in each regiment, and the colonels read aloud the following proclamation: "Soldiers, here is the battle you have so much desired. Now victory depends upon you: we must have it: it will give us abundance, good winter quarters and a prompt return to our country. Conduct yourselves as you did at Austerlitz, at Friedland, at Vitebsk, at Smolensk, and may the most distant posterity point to your conduct this day; may it be said of you: he was at the great battle under the walls of Moscow!" The soldiers responded with huzzahs; a cannon shot was fired and the battle began.

At the same signal the Imperial Guard and the staff officers left camp; we gathered near the redoubt taken the day before, and before which the Emperor posted himself. The attack became general all along the line, and for the first time the Emperor took no personal part in it. He remained a quarter league from the battlefield, receiving the reports of the generals and giving orders as well as they could be given from a distance. Never have I seen such furious fighting as on that day. There was scarcely any maneuvering; the attacks were made frontally and with great desperation. The First and Third Corps twice took the two redoubts on the left; the large redoubt on the right was taken by a regiment of cuirassiers, retaken by the enemy, and then seized anew by the First Division of the Third Corps detached for service with the Viceroy.[4] The Fourth Corps carried the village of Borodino and opposed the movement by the right wing of the Russian army to turn the position. I was dispatched at this time to the Viceroy, whom I found in the midst of his troops, and I was a witness to the valor with which he repulsed this attack. Each officer coming from the battlefield brought the news of some heroic action. Already we were victorious along the entire line. The Russians, driven from their positions and unable to retake them, were exposed for several hours to the fire of our artillery; by two o'clock they were only fighting to protect their retreat. It is said that Marshal Ney then asked the Emperor at least to advance the Young Guard in order to seal the victory; he refused, as he said later, because he did not wish to take any chances. General Kutusov retired during the evening. Our troops, overwhelmed with fatigue, could hardly follow. The army bivouacked on the battlefield.

The loss was heavy on both sides:[5] it can be placed at 28,000 French and 50,000 Russians. I might mention among those who fell on the enemy side Prince Eugene of Württemberg and Prince Bagration; on our side, General

---

[4] Eugene de Beauharnais, Josephine's son by a previous marriage. He became Viceroy of Italy in 1805. [Ed.]

[5] The losses of the French army were as follows: 10 generals killed, 39 wounded, total 49; 10 colonels killed, 27 wounded, total 37; 6,547 officers and men killed, and 21,453 wounded, total 28,000. During the battle the French army fired 60,000 cannon shots and used 1,400,000 musket cartridges.

Montbrun, commanding a corps of cavalry, and General Caulaincourt, brother of the Duke of Vicenza and aide-de-camp of the Emperor. This latter was much mourned at headquarters, where he had been greatly liked. He had been sent to replace General Montbrun, and had been killed in the large redoubt. A great number of officers of all ranks remained on the battlefield.

The next morning, the Fifth Corps moved to the right to march on Moscow by the old highway. General Kutusov, fearing he would be cut off, decided on a full retreat.

The Emperor went over the battlefield with us: it was horrible, and literally covered with dead. We saw all kinds of wounds and suffering; the Russian dead and wounded, however, were in far greater numbers than our own. The Emperor visited the wounded, had drink brought to them, and ordered that care be taken of them. The same day the army continued its movement, still in three columns, in the direction of Moscow. The taking of this city would complete our victory, and it was here that the Emperor expected to sign the peace. The Russian advance guard defended Mozhaisk for some time in order to set fire to it. Headquarters was established there on the 10th.

It was at this time that the Prince of Neuchâtel offered to suggest my name to the Emperor for the colonelcy of the Fourth Regiment of the line to replace Colonel Massy, killed in the battle. I accepted this offer gratefully, and being named the next day, I left Mozhaisk to join my new regiment.

Here I will end the first part of my account; in the part which follows I will write only the history of the Fourth Regiment, and of the Third Corps to which it belonged. I will say something, however, of the operations of the rest of the army, so that the reader will have an overall view of this momentous episode, and may judge the part which the Third Corps played in it.

PART TWO

Marshal Ney, General in Chief
General Gouré, Chief of Staff

Generals of Division	Brigadier Generals	Regiments	Colonels
First Division Ledru des Essarts	Gengoult Lenchantin Bruni	24th light 46th line 72nd line	Debellier Bru
Second Division Razout	Joubert D'Hénin	4th line 18th line 93rd line	Fezensac Pelleport Baudouin
Two Brigades of Light Cavalry	Beurmann Valmabelle		
Artillery	Fouchet		

CHAPTER ONE

Situation of the Third Corps

March from Mozhaisk to Moscow

Burning of the city

Position of the Third Corps

Entry into Moscow

Movements of the Russians

At Bogorodsk

Review of 18 October

Order for departure

I LEFT MOZHAISK ON THE MORNING of the 12th, and arrived that same evening at Marshal Ney's headquarters in a village near Kubinskoye; the regiments of the Third Corps were camped around the village. The Marshal welcomed me with all of his former kindness; I had served under him some years before, and I considered it a special favor to find myself under his orders again. The next morning I was received at the head of my regiment by General d'Hénin, the brigade commander.

This was the composition of the Third Corps (*see* chart on opposite page):

A third division of infantry composed of Württembergers, under the orders of General Marchand, was reduced to 1,000 men. The Prince of Württemberg commanded it at the beginning of the campaign. The Emperor reproached him severely on the depredations committed by his troops, depredations which were much exaggerated by the French. The Prince of Württemberg tried to establish a more rigorous discipline; but since they could only live through pillage, the starving soldiers wandered off. The Prince himself, ill and embittered, left the army.

Part Two, Chapter One

    The Fourth Regiment of the line had been formed in the first years of the Revolution, had participated in all the campaigns in Germany, and counted Joseph Bonaparte among its former colonels. At the time I took command the officers fell into three classes: The first, composed of ex-students fresh from the military school, had zeal and training but lacked experience and the hardiness to withstand the excessive rigors of the campaign. The second class, on the contrary, was made up of former non-commissioned officers whose total lack of formal training might have barred them from further advancement, but who had been promoted in order to spur emulation and to replace the enormous losses caused by such destructive campaigns; for the rest they were excellent soldiers, hardened to fatigue and knowing all that could be learned of war in the lower ranks. The third class came between the first two: it was composed of trained officers, mature in age, formed by experience and possessing the noble ambition to distinguish themselves and make their way. This class was unfortunately the least numerous.

    General Ledru had long been a colonel, and knew the service thoroughly in peace and war. General Razout, an old soldier, was so nearsighted that he could see nothing about him, and had to rely on those near him; his dispositions on the field of necessity reflected the constant uncertainty of which he was the victim. Among the brigadier generals I might mention General Joubert, an officer of passable merit, and General d'Hénin, whom a long captivity in England had made somewhat a stranger to war. The colonels were for the most part excellent soldiers. M. Pelleport, who had enlisted as a volunteer in **the Eighteenth, had received all of his promotions in this regiment, which he commanded with a rare distinction.**

    But the great advantage of the Third Corps was to be commanded by Marshal Ney, whose audacity, constancy,

Situation of the Third Corps

and admirable presence of mind I shall often have occasion to mention.

From the very first day I was struck by the exhaustion of the troops and their weakness in numbers. At army headquarters they only appreciated results, without thinking of what they cost, and they really had no idea of the state of the army; but in taking command of a regiment I had to treat matters of which I had been unaware, and I came to know the extent of the evil. The Fourth Regiment was reduced to 900 men out of the 2,800 which had crossed the Rhine; thus the four battalions now formed but two when mustered, and each company had a double complement of officers and non-commissioned officers. All of their equipment, and particularly their shoes, were in a dilapidated state. We still had then some flour and some herds of cattle and sheep; but these resources would soon be used up, and to replace them we would have to stay constantly on the move, for in twenty-four hours we completely stripped the country through which we passed.

What I have said of my regiment applies to all those in the Third Corps, and particularly the Württemberg Division, which was almost destroyed; thus, one could say with certainty that there remained but 8,000 combatants in an army corps of 25,000 men. There was a noticeable absence of officers wounded in recent engagements, among others the colonels of the Forty-sixth, Seventy-second, and Ninety-third. Never had we suffered such heavy losses; never had the morale of the army been so shaken. I no longer witnessed the former gaiety of the soldiers. A gloomy silence replaced the songs and jokes that had once made them forget the fatigue of the long marches. The officers themselves seemed worried; they now served only from a sense of duty and honor. This dejection, natural in a defeated army, was strange after a decisive engagement, after a victory which had opened the gates of Moscow to us.

The march continued in three columns, as before the battle: the King of Naples at the advance guard with the cavalry, then the First and Third Corps, the Imperial Guard, and headquarters; on the right, the Fifth Corps; on the left, the Fourth. The march was orderly, with the generals and officers at the head of their troops. General Kutusov, believing himself no longer able to defend Moscow, gradually withdrew his advance guard and retreated along the roads to Tver and Vladimir, thus uncovering the city. On the 13th the French army bivouacked at Perushkovo; the next day the advance guard entered Moscow. A horde of armed inhabitants tried briefly to defend the Kremlin but were soon dispersed; the advance guard went on beyond the city, while the Emperor established himself and the Guard at the Kremlin. The First and Third Corps camped a quarter league outside Moscow and were expressly prohibited from entering it. Thus it was only from a distance that we then contemplated that ancient capital which we had just conquered. Even so, we could admire its vast extent, its many colored domes, and the unbelievable variety of its many buildings. This day was a very happy one for us since it was to be the end of our labors, and since the victory on the Moskva and the taking of Moscow were to bring about peace. But at that very time an event unparalleled in the history of the world destroyed our fond hopes and showed how little we could count on a settlement with the Russians. Moscow, which they had been unable to defend, was put to the torch by their own hands. This great fire had long been planned. Governor Rostopchin had collected an immense quantity of combustible materials and incendiary rockets. He claimed that he was having built a balloon with which to burn the French army, and his proclamations, like those of General Kutusov, reassured the people of Moscow and made Russian defeats into victories: at Smolensk, the French had been beaten, at the Moskva they had been destroyed. If the Russian armies were retreating, it was to take up a better position and rendezvous with their reinforcements. All of this time the nobles were leaving Moscow, as well as the archives and treasures of the Kremlin; and when the Russian army stood at the gates of the city, it was no longer possible to hide the truth. Many inhabitants took flight; others stayed, confident that the French would find it in their interest to preserve Moscow.

On the morning of the 14th, the governor assembled three or four thousand men from the dregs of the population, among them liberated criminals; they were given matches and flares, and the police were ordered to conduct them throughout the city. The fire pumps were broken, and the departure of the civil authorities, who followed the army, was to be the signal for the fire. When the advance guard traversed the city they found it almost deserted. The inhabitants kept to their houses, waiting to see how we would decide their fate; but scarcely had the Emperor established himself in the Kremlin when the Bazaar, an immense building housing some 10,000 shops, burst into flames. The next day and for several days thereafter, fires were set in all the quarters. A violent wind drove the flames, and it was impossible to stop them, since the pumps had been destroyed. Those who were caught setting fires were shot on the spot. They said they were carrying out the governor's orders, and met their deaths with resignation. The houses were given over to pillage without hesitation, for what was carried off would have been consumed in the flames; but this pillage was accompanied by all the excesses which it engenders. The deluge of flames which we saw from our camp caused us lively

Part Two, Chapter One

concern, and I decided to seek news at headquarters. I entered the city alone, and soon the flames barred my way to the Kremlin. Yet neither this danger nor that posed by the collapse of houses could allay the thirst for plunder; the inhabitants, driven from their homes by the soldiers as often as by the flames, wandered about in the streets; some were seized by despair, while others evidenced a sad resignation. I returned to camp much affected by this spectacle, and I decided to give all my attention to my regiment and to turn my back on evils which I could not remedy.

I spent three days in the details of inspection: all the officers were presented to me individually, and I informed myself on the conduct and training of each. I also examined as far as circumstances would allow all that concerned the training and administration of the regiment. This was done in the light of the conflagration in Moscow. We had been forbidden to enter the city, but the pillage had begun, and since it was our only resource it was clear that those who came late would starve. I therefore agreed with the colonel of the Eighteenth that we would tacitly permit our soldiers to go and take part. Even so, it was only with the greatest difficulty that they obtained anything. On returning they had to traverse the camp of the First Corps placed in front of us, and they were obliged to fight with these soldiers or those of the Imperial Guard who wanted to plunder them in turn. No one profited less than ourselves from the sack of that city. After six days the fire died down for lack of fuel; nine-tenths of the city no longer existed. The Emperor, who had gone to the Petrovsky Palace during the fire, returned to the Kremlin to await the peace proposals on which he still counted.

But Czar Alexander, far from being discouraged by the loss of Moscow, saw it as a reason for pursuing the war with even greater vigor.

General Kutusov, thinking correctly that upon leaving Moscow we would move toward the southern provinces, left the Vladimir road and marched around Moscow, moving to the roads to Kaluga and Tula. This march, illuminated by the fires in Moscow, was a humiliating one for the Russian army. Kutusov placed himself behind the Nara, some twenty-five leagues from Moscow, and fortified this position with redoubts, thus protecting the roads to Kaluga and Tula. If we wished to penetrate the southern provinces we would thus be obliged to fight a second battle. In the meantime, the Russian army repaired its losses with new levies, organized its supplies, and took on a fresh courage with its new strength. Amidst these preparations there was only talk of peace along the picket lines, and a feigned interest in opening negotiations encouraged Napoleon in his hope of concluding peace. The King of Naples moved toward Kaluga with the advance guard, confronting the fortified camp of the Russians, and the Third Corps was ordered to replace him in the north on the roads to Tver and Vladimir where the enemy had left a corps of observation.

For the first time I passed through the ruins of Moscow at the head of my regiment. It was a spectacle at once very horrible and very bizarre. Some of the houses seemed to have been razed; others still possessed portions of wall, blackened with smoke; debris of all sorts filled the streets; a frightful odor rose from all sides. From time to time a cottage, a church, or a palace appeared still erect in the midst of this great disaster. The churches above all, by their domes of many colors, by the richness and variety of their construction, recalled the former opulence of Moscow. Most of the inhabitants had taken refuge there, having been driven by our soldiers from the houses which the fire had spared. These unfortunate creatures, dressed in rags, wandered like ghosts through the ruins. They were driven to the most desperate expedients in order to prolong their miserable existence. They devoured in the midst of the gardens the few vegetables that were still to be found, and they tore strips of flesh from the dead animals in the streets; we even saw them plunge into the river to get the wheat which the Russians had dumped into the water, and which had begun to ferment. During our march the roll of the drums and the sound of military music made this spectacle even more somber, for it gave the impression of a triumph in the midst of a scene of destruction, misery, and death.

After we had crossed the entirety of that immense city, we cantonned in the village along the road to Yaroslavl and Vladimir. I stayed at the chateau of Kuskova, which belonged to Count Sheremetev, a man of great wealth. This charming place had been pillaged like everything else. After we had consumed the few resources which this country offered, we returned to Moscow and took quarters in the Vladimir suburb. This district, on the north of Moscow, is traversed by a stream called the Yauza, which empties into the Moskva in the middle of the city. Most of the houses were separated by cultivation plots and gardens. A few mansions could be seen there as in other quarters; the rest were built of wood. Since nearly everything was burned, we had to place the companies some distance from one another in spite of the problems it presented for the distribution of rations, and especially for police and discipline. I lodged in the midst of my regiment with the senior officers, in a large stone house that was largely undamaged. Forty inhabitants of the neighborhood had taken refuge in a large room in this house. I gave orders that they be protected and their misery alleviated with the means we had. But what could we do for them? We scarcely had enough for ourselves. It was difficult to obtain black bread and beer; meat was becoming very scarce. We had to send out large detachments to find the cattle in the forests where the peasants had hidden them, and very often the detachments came back in the evening empty-handed. Such was the so-called abundance which the looting of this city brought us. We had liqueurs, sugar, and preserves, while we lacked meat and bread. We covered ourselves with furs, but we no longer had uniforms or shoes. While we had diamonds, gems, and all manner of luxuries, we were on the brink of starvation. A large number of Russian soldiers were wandering about the streets. I had fifty arrested and taken to headquarters. A general to whom I reported told me that I should have had them shot, and authorized me to do so in the future. I did not take advantage of this authorization.

It would be no difficult task to show what disorders and misfortunes attended our stay in Moscow. Each officer, each soldier could relate bizarre anecdotes on this subject. One of the most touching was that concerning a Russian whom a French officer found hidden in the ruins of a house. He made him understand by signs that he would protect him, and led him off. Later, when he was obliged to deliver an order, the officer saw one of his comrades leading a squad and turned the prisoner over to him, saying very forcefully to him: "This gentleman will take care of you." This latter officer, mistaking the meaning of these words and the tone in which they were spoken, took the unfortunate for an arsonist and had him shot.

At the beginning of the fire a very young man, German in origin and a student in medicine, took refuge in my quarters; he was nearly naked and seemed to have lost his mind. I took him in and kept him in my quarters for nearly three weeks; he seemed to be grateful, but nothing could allay his terror. One day I proposed in jest that he enroll in my regiment; that same evening he disappeared, and I never saw him again.

Meanwhile the Russian army steadily strengthened

Part Two, Chapter One

itself along the banks of the Nara. The groups of partisans around Moscow became more audacious. The town of Vereya was surprised and the garrison massacred. The detachments and convoys which were coming to join the army and the wounded and sick who were being transported to the rear were attacked along the road to Smolensk; the Cossacks attacked our foragers at the very gates of Moscow; the peasants killed isolated stragglers. The King of Naples, whose cavalry had been almost completely destroyed and long since reduced to living on horsemeat, repeated constantly that we should make peace or retire. But the Emperor refused to see or to listen to anyone; in response to their representations, the generals received from headquarters the most bizarre orders. They were to re-establish order in Moscow and protect the peasants who would bring food to the market, though the region was already despoiled and the peasants armed against us; or again, they were to buy 10,000 horses in a country where there were no longer either horses or inhabitants; later there was a plan for us to pass the winter in a ravaged town, where we starved during the month of October. Then came the order to have shoes and winter clothes made in each regiment; and when the colonels complained that there was not enough cloth or leather, they were told that they had but to look about to obtain what was needed. At the same time, as if to render this order even more incapable of execution, pillage was rigorously forbidden, and the Imperial Guard was consigned to the Kremlin. A governor, an intendant, and an administrator were appointed. A whole month passed while our situation did no improve in the slightest.

About the 10th of October, a division of the Fourth Corps made a movement toward Dmitrov, on the road to Tver. Meanwhile Marshal Ney seized Bogorodsk, a dozen leagues from Moscow on the road to Vladimir. Some days were spent in building barracks about this little town

At Bogorodsk

in which to spend the winter. This ruse was useless; it impressed neither the enemy nor our soldiers. I did not go to Bogorodsk. At that time I participated in an expedition commanded by General Marchand along the banks of the Klyasma between the road to Vladimir and that to Tver. A part of my regiment accompanied me, the remainder had followed Marshal Ney. The enemy, faithful to his plan, retired at our approach. General Marchand had a blockhouse built on the Klyasma at a spot where a post had been overrun by a regiment of Cossacks. The command of this fort had just been given to a very able officer when General Marchand suddenly received orders to return with his entire detachment. It was easy then to guess that the army was going to abandon Moscow, since its approaches were no longer to be guarded.

During the course of this expedition I found everywhere the same misery. The generals collected some provisions, but there were no resources for the army. The peasants hid their food and did not dare produce it even when we promised to pay them. A soldier of my regiment, the son of a farmer on the Côte-d'Or, died beside me in front of the campfire. This young man had languished for a long time; a slow fever caused by fatigue and bad food consumed him. He died of exhaustion, and after having assured myself that he was dead, I had him buried at the foot of a tree. We found in his knapsack some letters from his mother which were very touching in their simplicity. I sincerely regretted the death of this unfortunate, doomed to die far from his country and from a family that loved him. Such misfortunes were common among us, and I recount this death which I witnessed only because this sad spectacle was like a presage of all the calamities which were to fall upon us. The detachment returned to Moscow on the 15th.

Two days passed without a word said about our departure. On the 18th the Emperor reviewed the Third Corps in the Kremlin square. This review was as splendid as circumstances permitted. The colonels strove to surpass one another in presenting their regiments in good condition. No one who saw them could guess how much they had endured, or how much they were to suffer. I am sure that the fine appearance of our army in the midst of this vast desolation reinforced the obstinacy of the Emperor, convincing him that with such soldiers nothing was impossible. All of the Third Corps present there did not number 10,000 men. During this review M. de Bérenger, aide-de-camp of the King of Naples, brought the Emperor news of the affair at Vinkovo, where our troops had been surprised and forced to retire the day before. This combat brought to an end a sort of armistice which had existed at the advance posts: it marked the end of any kind of agreement and was to hasten our departure. The Emperor's concern was evident in his look. He hastened the review, although he named men to all the vacant posts and awarded many decorations. He was now more than ever in need of those means by which he knew so well how to draw superhuman efforts from his army. I took advantage of his generosity to obtain rewards for those of my officers whose devotion had been proven to me: many of them were promoted.[1] The general who commanded the Württemberg Division under General Marchand was created a count of the Empire, with a gift of 20,000 francs—a meager reward indeed for the sufferings of 12,000 men whom exhaustion and privation had now reduced to eight hundred.

The review was hardly over before the colonels received the order to depart on the following day. When I

---

1 M. d'Arcine, Adjutant-Major, was named battalion chief. He later took part in the expedition to Algiers in 1830 as a *maréchal de camp*.

Order for departure

returned to my quarters I ordered preparations made, and had what was left of our food loaded into carts. I left in my house the flour which I could not take. I had been advised to destroy it; but I could not bring myself to deprive the miserable inhabitants, and I gave it to them gladly as a recompense for the harm that we had been obliged to do them. I was touched and grateful for the blessings they gave me: perhaps this brought me luck.

CHAPTER TWO

Plans of the Emperor

Departure from Moscow

March to Borovsk

Operations of the other corps

Combat at Maloyaroslavets

Retreat toward Smolensk

March from Borovsk to Mozhaisk

From Mozhaisk to Vyazma

Situation of the army

Affair at Vyazma

THE EMPEROR HAD ABANDONED all hope of peace, and now thought only of retreat. He had to recross the Dvina and the Dnieper, re-establish communications on the left with the Second and Sixth Corps, and on the right with the Seventh and the Austrians, who were defending the Grand Duchy of Warsaw. The Smolensk route, which had been completely devastated, offered us no resources; it was decided to head toward Kaluga, and by taking the road to Borovsk and Maloyaroslavets, to turn the enemy's position in his fortified camp. By this means the imprudence of our long stay in Moscow might be redeemed. Victory would open the road to the southern provinces, or at least it would permit us to retire through Roslavl toward Moghilev, or toward Smolensk by way of Medyn and Elnya, through country that had not been touched by war.

Already the Fourth Corps had occupied Fominskoye, on the old road to Kaluga; it was to be the advance guard and strike the first blows. Meanwhile, as he was departing, the Emperor decided to leave in Moscow the mark of his vengeance by completing the destruction of what had escaped the fury of the Russians. Marshal Mortier was ordered to remain behind for several days with the Young Guard in order to protect the march of the other detachments from enemy forces along the road from the north. At the same time he was to blow up the Kremlin and set fire to what remained. Thus was completed the extinction of this unfortunate city, burned by its own inhabitants and ravaged and destroyed by its conquerors. The manner in which the Marshal modified this terrible order, and the care he took of the wounded and ill amid this frightful devastation, pay honor to his heart as well as to his character.

On the night of the 18th of October the baggage train of the Third Corps moved to the Seminov convent, designated as the assembly point. Never had we hauled so many vehicles behind us. Each company had at least a cart or a sled to carry its food; the night was barely sufficient to load them and place them in order. An hour before dawn the companies assembled in front of my quarters and we departed. There was something lugubrious about that march. The darkness of the night, the silence of our movement, the smoking ruins which we trampled underfoot, all of this seemed to fill the imagination with sadness. Thus each of us recorded with misgiving the beginning of that memorable retreat. The soldiers themselves felt very keenly the difficulty of our situation: they were endowed with that intelligence and that admirable instinct which distinguish the French soldier, and which, in revealing the extent of the danger, seems also to redouble the courage necessary to overcome it.

The convent of Seminov, situated near the Kaluga Gate, was in flames when we arrived. They were burning rations which they could not carry off; and by an oversight that was typical of the times, the colonels had not been notified. There was still space in many of the wagons, and yet we watched the burning of provisions that might have saved our lives.

The Third Corps, now assembled, marched along the new Kaluga road along with the First Corps and the Imperial Guard. My regiment numbered 1,100 men at this period, and the Third Corps did not exceed 11,000. I believe that the total strength of the army when it left Moscow could be placed at 100,000 men.

Nothing was more curious than the march of this army, and the broad plains which we encountered on leaving Moscow enabled us to observe it in all its details. We hauled behind us all that had escaped the fire. The most elegant and magnificent carriages mingled with wagons, *drozhkis*, and the carts which hauled the food. These vehicles, moving in several columns along the wide roads of Russia, presented the appearance of an immense caravan. From a hilltop I watched for a long time this spectacle which recalled the wars of the conquerors of Asia; the plain was covered with this huge procession, and the steeples of Moscow on the horizon completed the picture. We were brought to a halt here, as if to let us contemplate for the last time the ruins of this antique city, which soon vanished from our view.

After two days' march the Third Corps arrived at Chirkovo, and took up position there guarding the junction of the roads from Podolsk and Fominskoye, while the First Corps and the Guard moved successively by rapid march along the old Kaluga road, so as to support the Fourth. The Third Corps, which was to execute this movement last, spent three days in the position at Chirkovo, and left at midnight on the 23rd. This night march was frightful: the rain fell in torrents and the roads were completely ruined. We did not arrive at Borovsk until the evening of the 26th. During this march we were continually harassed by the Cossacks, although they did not

Combat at Maloyaroslavets

dare attempt any serious enterprise against us. I took great care to maintain order, discipline, and exactitude in our regiment; I had nothing but praise for the officers and men. Only a single sergeant (a good soldier, moreover) showed some negligence in the command of an advanced post that I had given him: I ordered that he be broken in spite of the pleas of his captain. Generals Girardin and Beurmann flanked our march with light cavalry. They had received the order to burn all the villages.

We rejoined headquarters at Borovsk, and it was here that we learned of recent events. General Kutusov, having learned of the march of the French army along the old Kaluga road, had left his camp at Tarutino; a rapid march parallel to our own brought him to Maloyaroslavets, where he met and attacked the Fourth Corps. In this brilliant engagement the French secured the advantage in spite of their smaller number. But Kutusov was now six leagues away in a position defended by redoubts; already one of his divisions was attempting to move around our right along the Medyn road. We thus had to offer battle or retreat. The situation was grave, the moment decisive. Marshal Bessières and the other generals favored retreat; it was not that they doubted our victory, but they feared the losses the battle would cause, and the disorganization which would result. The cavalry and artillery horses were weakened by fatigue and poor fodder. How could we replace those we would lose? How would we transport the artillery, the munitions, and the wounded? In this situation a march toward Kaluga would be risky indeed, and prudence dictated a retreat toward Smolensk. Count Lobau, in fact, said on several occasions that we had not a moment to lose in regaining the Niemen. Napoleon hesitated for a long time: he spent the whole day of the 25th examining the battlefield and talking with the generals. Finally he decided upon retreat, and it must be said to his credit that one of the considerations that swayed him was the fact that we would have had to abandon our wounded after the battle. The whole army took the road to Smolensk by way of Mozhaisk, and the movement began when the Third Corps arrived at Borovsk. The First Corps provided the rear guard. The Cossacks continued to harass us with their usual energy: they attacked the baggage train of the Fourth Corps, that of headquarters, and finally the Emperor himself, whose escort put them to flight. The roads were encumbered with vehicles of all kinds which continually impeded our movement; we encountered swollen streams which we had to cross on a few planks or by fording. On the morning of the 28th the Third Corps occupied Vereya, and reached Gorodok-Borisov the same evening; on the 29th, passing the ruins of Mozhaisk on our right, we reached the high road below this city.

One can easily imagine what hardships awaited our army in the regions which had been steadily ravaged by French and Russians. If a few houses still stood, they were without inhabitants. Our nearest provisions were in Smolensk, at some eighty leagues' distance. Until we reached Smolensk we could expect neither flour, nor meat, nor forage. We were reduced to the provisions we had brought from Moscow; but these provisions, none too plentiful in themselves, had the further disadvantage of being unevenly distributed, as is often the case with the fruits of pillage. One regiment had preserved some cattle but lacked bread; another had flour but not meat. Even within the same regiment this disparity could be seen: some companies were dying of hunger while others lived amid abundance. The commanders ordered that they share alike, but the self-interest of the soldiers led them to evade surveillance and defy authority. What is more, in order to preserve our food we had to preserve the horses which hauled it, and the lack of forage caused a great number of these to die every day.

The soldiers who left the road to seek food fell into the hands of Cossacks or armed peasants. The road itself was littered with caissons which had been blown up, and with cannon and vehicles abandoned when the horses no longer had the strength to pull them. From the very first days, indeed, this retreat resembled a rout. The Emperor continued to take his vengeance upon the houses. The Prince of Eckmühl, commanding the rear guard, was ordered to burn everything, and never was an order carried out with greater exactitude and thoroughness. Detachments sent to the left and right of the road burned the chateaux and villages at as great a distance as the enemy's pursuit would permit. The spectacle of this destruction was not the most horrible of those which we beheld: a column of Russian prisoners marched in front of us, guarded by troops from the Confederation of the Rhine. They were given nothing but a little horsemeat, and the soldiers charged with escorting them killed those who could no longer march. Along the road we encountered their cadavers, all of which had their skulls shattered. In all justice I should say that my soldiers were outraged at this; they sensed, moreover, that this barbarity would subject those who fell into the hands of the enemy to cruel reprisals.

As we passed through the village of Borodino some of the officers went to visit the Moskva battlefield. They found debris still littering the terrain, and the dead of both armies still lying where they had been struck down. It was said that they found wounded soldiers still clinging to life; I can hardly believe this, and no proof of it was ever made. On the evening of the 29th we reached the Kolotsk Abbey, which had earlier been transformed into a hospital, but which was now nothing more than a vast cemetery. A lone building which still stood among the ruins of the town of Gzhatsk also served as a hospital for our sick. The colonels were given the order to go there and identify the men of their regiments. The patients had been left without medicines, without food, and without any help. It was all I could do to enter amid the filth of every description which filled the stairs, the corridors, and the rooms. I found three men from my regiment there, and I was very happy that I could rescue them.

On November 1 we arrived at Vyazma. A few huts situated in the Moscow suburb[1] served us as lodgings; this shelter, wretched as it was, seemed very commodious to us after fifteen days of bivouac.

Meanwhile, as soon as General Kutusov perceived the retrograde movement of the French army, he sent in pursuit General Miloradovich with a sizeable body of troops and all the Cossacks of Platov, while he himself led the main Russian army along the Elnya road in order to arrive at the Dnieper before us. General Miloradovich, whose advance guard pressed the First Corps, marched parallel to the road, and sustained his troops in country less ravaged than that which we were passing through. The back roads which this force used also had the advantage of being more direct than the highway and gave the enemy the opportunity to strike our rear guard and to reach Vyazma ahead of us. In this situation the Emperor was much criticized for not marching fast enough, yet the men and especially the horses were overcome with exhaustion. To hasten our march we would have had to sacrifice all our baggage. No doubt this step

---

[1] That is, in the suburb of Vyazma situated along the road to Moscow. I will explain here this manner of expression that will be used again; thus at Smolensk, the Moscow, Petersburg, and Vilna suburbs designated the roads along which the suburbs were located, and similarly in other towns.

would have spared us much difficulty, but we could not yet accept such an extreme measure. Finally, on November 3, General Miloradovich brought his troops to the highway about a league from Vyazma, and fiercely attacked the Fourth Corps which was marching toward the town. By this maneuver the Fourth Corps and the First which followed it found themselves cut off and obliged to fight their way through an enemy superior in cavalry and artillery. At the same time another Russian division sought to seize Vyazma by the Medyn Road. Fortunately Marshal Ney, who was still in the town, had taken measures to prevent such a stroke. Two small streams, the Vlitza and the Vyazma, form a semi-circle around the town on the side toward Medyn and make its defense easy. The Ledru Division took up a position on the plateau which dominates these streams and checked the enemy's efforts to force a passage. The Razout Division advanced up the Moscow road to aid the First and Fourth Corps. After a fierce battle which lasted five hours, these two corps pierced the enemy line and restored their communications with us.

We returned to the suburb, and I learned that the Third Corps was to relieve the First in the rear guard. This difficult and important task could not have been confided to a general more capable of carrying it out than Marshal Ney, and I may add that we seconded him with all our zeal. The good account which my regiment had just given of itself on this day filled me with confidence. I informed my officers of the difficult and glorious task which had been given us; and while the First and Fourth Corps passed through Vyazma and left us in the presence of the enemy, we prepared ourselves to be worthy replacements, knowing that at stake were our honor, the renown of our troops, and the salvation of the whole army.

CHAPTER THREE

Assigned to the rear guard

Departure from Vyazma

March to Dorogobuzh

Affair at Slopnevo

Intense cold

Arrival at Smolensk

Operations of the other corps

UP TO THIS TIME THE THIRD Corps, which had been far from the rear guard and little harassed by the enemy's light troops, had only to struggle against exhaustion and hunger; now we were to withstand alone the assaults of the Russian army, and to struggle against death in many guises. One may ask whether patience and courage had ever been put to such tests.

On November 4 the Third Corps left Vyazma to take up a position along a forest bordering the stream of the same name where it crosses the road to Smolensk. The wise choice of this position and the firm resolve of our troops kept the enemy from crossing the Vyazma. All day long they directed their attacks against our right along the Medyn road; General Beurmann, who commanded here, held until the evening. Two companies from my regiment shared the honor of this fine defense. Meanwhile the Fourth and First Corps passed through our ranks in the greatest disorder. I could scarcely believe that they had suffered so much, and that their disorganization was so far advanced. Only the Italian Royal Guard still marched in good

Departure from Vyazma

order; the rest seemed demoralized and overwhelmed with exhaustion. A great number of men who had lost their units marched in a disorganized mob, most of them without arms; many of them spent the night with us in the Vyazma forest. I tried to get them to go on without waiting for the rear guard. It was important for them to gain a few hours' march. At the same time we did not want them to become mixed in our ranks and hamper our movements. Thus their own best interest was ours too; but fatigue or laziness made them deaf to our advice. Dawn had scarcely come when the Third Corps took up its arms and began its march. Then all the stragglers left their camps and joined us. Those who were wounded or ill remained about the fires, imploring us not to leave them to the enemy. We had no means of transporting them, and we had to pretend that we did not hear these pleas which we could not heed. As for the horde of stragglers who had abandoned their colors, even though they could still fight I ordered that they be driven off with blows of our musket stocks, and I warned them that if the enemy attacked us, I would fire into them should they give us the least difficulty.

The First Division marched in the van, the Second in the rear guard, with each division formed so that its left led the march. Thus my regiment was the extreme rear guard. Squads of cavalry and infantry covered our flanks; when we left the forest, a vast plain permitted them to spread out and parallel our march. The officers and generals, each at his post, directed the movements. The enemy, who had followed us all day without attempting anything, tried in the evening to attack the rear guard in the Semlevo defile; my regiment contained the Russian advance guard with the aid of two cannon, and thus gave the other troops time to pass through the defile. We went through in turn, leaving in the presence of the enemy two

Part Two, Chapter Three

companies of *voltigeurs* who did not rejoin us until the middle of the night; the Third Corps camped on the heights just beyond. We had scarcely settled down to rest when the Russians began to throw shells into our camp. One of them struck a tree under which I was sleeping. No one was wounded, and there was only some momentary disorder in a few companies of the Eighteenth. I have always observed that shots fired at night do little harm, but they do stir the imagination and make the soldiers think that the enemy is prodigiously active.

The next day's march was only briefly interrupted by an unsuccessful attempt which the Cossacks made upon our baggage train; after covering three leagues, the Third Corps took up a position near Postvia-Dvor. The Emperor desired to march slowly so as to preserve the baggage. In vain did Marshal Ney write him that there was no time to lose, that the enemy was pressing the rear guard, that the Russian army was moving along our flank by forced marches, and that there were genuine grounds for concern that it would reach Orsha or Smolensk before us. As for us, this day enabled us to recover from the exertions of the day before; we bivouacked on the edge of a forest that provided a good campsite. The weather was good and very temperate for the season, and we hoped easily to reach Smolensk, which was to mark the end of our fatigues. During the next day's march the weather changed suddenly and became very cold. It was late when we arrived in Dorogobuzh. The First Division was placed on the heights of the town; the Second stopped a quarter league before it to defend the approaches. The night was the coldest we had yet experienced. Snow fell in abundance, and the violence of the wind kept us from lighting fires; moreover, the brush in which we bivouacked gave us little fuel for our camps.

Meanwhile Marshal Ney had decided to hold the ene-

Affair at Slopnevo

my before Dorogobuzh all of the next day. We were still some twenty-one leagues from Smolensk, and halfway to this city we would have to cross the Dnieper; it was important, therefore, to avoid any difficulties at this point and to give the army we were protecting the time to cross it with its artillery and baggage.

At daybreak on the 8th, the Fourth and Eighteenth Regiments under General Joubert left their camps to take positions in Dorogobuzh; the Cossacks, favored by a thick mist, harassed us until we entered the town.

Dorogobuzh, which stands on a height, is on the Dnieper. The Second Division, which was charged with defending it, was disposed as follows: two cannon in battery at the entrance of the lower street, supported by a post of the Fourth Regiment; on the left a company of the Eighteenth on the Dnieper bridge; on the right atop a height and in front of a church, a hundred men of the Fourth, commanded by a *chef de bataillon*; the rest of the division in the courtyard of the chateau located on the same height. The First Division was in reserve behind the town. Soon the enemy infantry appeared and began the attack: the Dnieper bridge was taken and the post before the church was seized. General Razout, who stayed in the courtyard with the rest of the division, was troubled with his customary indecision. We were about to be surrounded when he finally gave us the order to march. There was not a moment to lose. I flung my regiment forward at a charge, and we threw ourselves on the enemy, who was occupying the heights of the town. The fighting was very fierce; the nature of the terrain and the snow in which we sank up to our knees forced us to disperse and fight hand-to-hand. The advance of the Russians was halted, but soon the enemy penetrated again into the lower town, and General Razout, who feared being cut off, ordered retreat. I retired slowly, reforming squads and always facing the enemy; the Eighteenth, which had seconded our efforts, followed this movement. The two regiments left the enemy master of the town and reformed behind the First Division.

Marshal Ney, very angry at the ill success of his plan, blamed General Razout, General Joubert, and everyone else. He claimed that the enemy was not in sufficient force to have chased us from Dorogobuzh in such a fashion, and he asked me how many I had seen; I took the liberty of telling him that we had been too close to them to be able to count them. Before deciding to leave, he even ordered General d'Hénin to re-enter the lower town with the Ninety-third and retake some caissons. Hardly had this regiment begun its movement when the Russian artillery disrupted its ranks and drove it back. Marshal Ney was obliged to abandon any further attempt; once again he took the road to Smolensk.

During this time the privations to which we had been subjected since the beginning of the retreat became more severe; the few provisions which we had were now becoming exhausted. The horses which drew them were dying of hunger and overwork, and were themselves eaten by the soldiers. Since we had been in the rear guard all the men who strayed from the road in search of food fell into the hands of the enemy, whose pursuit became more and more vigorous. The severe cold added much to our hardships and sufferings. Many soldiers completely exhausted, threw down their arms and left the ranks in order to march at their own pace. They stopped wherever they could find a piece of firewood and cooked a little horsemeat or bread, if indeed their own comrades did not take this last resource from them; for our soldiers seized forcibly the food of all the stragglers they encountered, and the latter could consider themselves for-

Intense cold

tunate if their clothes were not taken as well. After having ravaged the entire countryside, we were reduced to preying upon one another, and this extreme measure was a necessary one. We had at all costs to preserve the soldiers who remained with their colors, and who alone withstood in the rear guard the assaults of the enemy. The stragglers who no longer belonged to a regiment and could no longer do service had no right to any pity. Thus the road we travelled resembled a battlefield. Those who had resisted cold weather and exhaustion succumbed to the torments of hunger; those who had preserved a little food were too weak to keep up with the march and were taken by the enemy; some had their limbs frozen and died in the snow; others fell asleep in villages and were consumed in the fires lighted by their comrades. At Dorogobuzh I saw a soldier from my regiment upon whom privation produced the effects of drunkenness. He stayed among us without recognizing us; he asked us where his regiment was, and called the names of the soldiers in his company, and then spoke to them as though they were strangers; his walk was unsteady and his look distracted. He disappeared at the beginning of the engagement and I never saw him again. Several *cantinières*[1] and wives of soldiers belonging to regiments that had preceded us found themselves among us. Several of these unfortunates had children with them; and in spite of the self-concern that was so common then, everyone hastened to help them. The drum major carried a child in his arms for a long time. The officers who had kept a horse shared it with these poor people. For several days a woman and her child rode in a cart which I still had; but what could such feeble assistance do in the face of so

---

[1] The *cantinières* were female sutlers who travelled with the army and supplied the soldiers with tobacco, wine, and the like. [Ed.]

much suffering, and how could we alleviate the misery from which we ourselves suffered?

From Dorogobuzh we reached in two days Slopnevo, on the banks of the Dnieper. The road was so slippery that the badly-shod horses could hardly stand. That night we camped in the snow amid the trees of a forest. Each regiment took its turn in the extreme rear guard which the enemy pursued and harassed unceasingly. The army continued to march so slowly that we ran into the First Corps, which was marching ahead of us. The overcrowding at the Dnieper bridge in Slopnevo had been extreme. For a quarter league in front of it the road was covered with abandoned wagons and caissons. On the morning of the 10th, before we crossed the stream, we worked to clear the bridge and burn all these vehicles. We found several bottles of rum which were of great help. I was in the rear guard, and all day my regiment defended the road leading to the bridge. The woods through which this road passes were filled with wounded whom we had to leave behind, and whom the Cossacks massacred almost in our midst. M. Rouchat, a second lieutenant, imprudently approached a caisson that was being destroyed, and he was blown to pieces by the explosion. Toward evening our troops crossed the Dnieper and the bridge was destroyed.

It was now important to prevent the enemy's passage of the stream, for we were only eleven leagues from Smolensk. We had to allow the troops preceding us sufficient time to reach this city and prepare its defense. The Emperor did not even expect the Third Corps at Smolensk for some four or five days, so little idea did he have of the situation of the army and particularly of the rear guard.

Marshal Ney made his dispositions to defend the passage. The Fourth Regiment was placed on the bank of the stream, the Eighteenth in the second line. The Marshal established his headquarters in a heavily-palisaded blockhouse built to guard the bridge. He placed General d'Hénin with the Ninety-third in the village of Pnevo, a quarter league to the left, and the First Division along the Dnieper on the extreme right. In the evening he spent a long time strolling in front of my regiment with General Joubert and myself. He pointed out to us the unfortunate consequences of the engagement at Dorogobuzh. The enemy had gained a day, had hastened our retreat, and had compelled us to abandon our caissons, our baggage, and our wounded; all of these misfortunes would have been avoided if we had defended Dorogobuzh for twenty-four hours. General Joubert spoke of the debility of our troops, and of their discouragement. The Marshal replied heatedly that it was simply a matter of getting killed, and that a glorious death was too fine a thing for anyone to avoid the opportunity. As for myself, I was content to say that I had left the heights of Dorogobuzh only after having twice received the order.

On the morning of the 11th the enemy infantry approached the opposite bank and began an engagement with the Fourth Regiment. The attack was so spirited and so unexpected that bullets were falling in our camps before the soldiers had time to seize their arms. The skirmishers went forward to the edge of the stream to return the enemy's fire, but the nature of the terrain, covered with brush on the opposite bank and absolutely clear on ours, made the fight too unequal. The Second Battalion entered the blockhouse, and the First took to a grove of trees which afforded some shelter; the fusillade continued between the Russian infantry and the battalion in the blockhouse. The Marshal spent the whole day there, directing the fire of the soldiers and firing several shots himself; I took up position there too, believing it my duty to command directly the portion of my regiment which was most exposed. Toward evening the Russians crossed the Dnieper near the village occupied by the Ninety-third and maneuvered so as to envelop it. General d'Hénin left his position and returned to the blockhouse, and this brought him a stern reprimand from Marshal Ney. He was in truth very severe. In war an officer commanding a detached body must know how to reach decisions without waiting for orders which may not reach him. He will be accused of weakness if he retires; he will be accused of recklessness if he compromises the troops confided to him. To accept injustice is one of the duties of a military career, and assuredly one of the most painful. For the rest, the memory of this reprimand which General d'Hénin retained came close to being very disastrous for us, as I shall explain later.

The next day, the 12th, the Third Corps began its march again at five o'clock in the morning. I continued to defend the blockhouse until seven, and then rejoined the column, after having set fire to the blockhouse as I had been expressly ordered to do. This rage to burn everything included even the palisade, and this brought us misfortune; the enemy, informed of our departure by the smoke, fired shells which struck several men.

There were still two days of march before we reached Smolensk. Those two days were fully as difficult as the preceding ones. The Cossacks harassed us unceasingly, and even attempted a serious attack on the Eighteenth Regiment, though without success. On the 13th we had to cover seven leagues over icy roads and in intense cold. The violence of the wind was such that when we halted we could not remain in one place; repose thus became another kind of fatigue. Finally in the evening we came within a half league of Smolensk and took up positions in the ravines which defended the approaches to it. The night brought our sufferings to the utmost limit, as a fitting end to this cruel retreat. Several soldiers froze to death in the camp, and others had their limbs frozen. At daybreak we perceived with great joy the towers of Smolensk, which we had long regarded as the end of our miseries, since the army was to find repose here, and an abundance of those provisions of which we had been so long deprived.

These hopes were far from being realized, however; on every hand fortune seemed to favor the Russians. On the Dvina, General Wittgenstein, after having carried Polotsk on the 18th of October, was seeking to drive the Second and Sixth Corps down the road to Smolensk. The Ninth Corps was dispatched from this city to give them assistance. At the other extremity of the theater of war, the peace concluded with Turkey had permitted Admiral Chichagov, commander of the army of Moldavia, to join the corps of Tormasov. The Austrians had retired behind the Bug, and the Admiral was moving in rapid marches to seize Minsk, where we had great storehouses, and to bar our passage of the Beresina.

During this time the main Russian army was constantly maneuvering on our flanks, intercepting communications, overwhelming detached bodies of troops, and preventing us from leaving the road. On the left the brigade of General Augereau was surrounded near Elnya and laid down its arms. On the right the Fourth Corps, which had marched from Dorogobuzh toward Vitebsk, had suffered great depredations from the cold, the wretched roads, and the pursuit of the enemy. Nearly all of its artillery was lost in the crossing of the Vop, and this corps retired in all haste to Smolensk, where it arrived on the same day as the Third. It had become impossible to halt at Smolensk. We had to hurry to precede the enemy to the Beresina, and reunite ourselves with the Second and Ninth Corps in the process. The order was given to continue the march, despite the rigors of the season and the deplorable condition of the troops. The Third Corps, ever faithful in fulfilling its noble task, remained charged with the rear guard; we prepared to meet new fatigues with new force, and new dangers with a new courage.

CHAPTER FOUR

Departure of the army

Conduct of Marshal Ney

Fighting in the suburbs

Devastation of the city

Departure of the Third Corps

Affairs at Krasnii

Separated from the rest of the arm

Arrival at Krasnii

SMOLENSK, ALONG WITH MINSK, was one of the major supply depots of the army. We had hoped to provide for our most pressing needs by drawing on the stores that had been assembled there, and indeed they might well have sufficed us; but when disorganization had begun in such a large army, it became almost impossible to arrest its progress. The administrators and the employees of every description who were charged with the army's logistical services were no longer anything but elements of disorder, and the evil was only compounded by all the efforts made to correct it. The passage of the army through Smolensk offered a tragic example of this. Since the taking of the city, General Charpentier, the Governor, and M. de Villeblanche, the Intendant of the province, had made every effort to restore the confidence of the population. Thanks to their attentions, seconded by the good discipline of the Ninth Corps, the rebuilding of the houses had begun, and food was being brought into the city and stored, when suddenly hordes of our soldiers came pouring through the gates, hoping to find rest and plenty at Smolensk.

Napoleon, fearing the tumult that would be caused by all these stragglers and by the regiments, which were scarcely more disciplined, had hurried there with the Imperial Guard. He forbade anyone to enter, and ordered the regiments to settle in the suburbs. The Guard received provisions of all sorts in abundance, but when they tried to aid the other troops, the disorder of the administration, which equalled that of the troops, kept any effective measures from being taken. Abuses of all sorts took place unpunished; the storehouses were broken into and pillaged, and as is always the case, the provisions for several months were destroyed in twenty-four hours. The soldiers pillaged and died of hunger. The Third Corps, which arrived last under the walls of Smolensk, and was still occupied with defending its approaches, was forgotten by those whom it protected. While we still faced the enemy the other corps completed the looting of the depots. When I entered the city I could find nothing for my regiment or for myself. Thus we had to continue our retreat without having received any assistance.

To the Third Corps were added the 129th Regiment and a regiment of Illyrians who were shared by the two divisions. This reinforcement was very necessary. Since Moscow the 11,000 men of the Third Corps had been reduced to less than 3,000. The Württemberg Division and the cavalry no longer existed; the artillery had preserved only a few cannon; and it was with these slender forces that we had to face the Russian advance guard. Already the army had taken the road to Orsha, and Marshal Ney, who remained, prepared to defend the city as long as possible in order to delay the enemy's pursuit. I spoke of Smolensk at the beginning of this account. I said that this city was situated on the left bank of the Dnieper, and that a solitary suburb lay in the form of an amphitheater on the right bank; the Petersburg and Moscow roads pass through this suburb. At the period of which I am speaking now it had been almost completely burned. A bridge thrown across the Dnieper led into the city, and a strong bridgehead built on the right bank guarded the passage.

On the morning of the 14th the Third Corps withdrew from the approaches to Smolensk, and was placed as follows: the Second Division in the suburb on the right bank; the First in reserve at the bridgehead; the Fourth Regiment guarded the Moscow gate, and the Illyrian Regiment, the Petersburg one. We occupied the few houses which the fire had spared. The cold was so extreme that on the preceding night the soldiers at the advance posts had threatened to leave them and return to the houses. I sent some good officers to remind them of their duty, firmly decided to go there myself if my presence were necessary, and to encamp with all the officers of my regiment. It was a point of honor, since the defense of the entrance to the suburb had been confided to my regiment, and a surprise would have endangered the entire division. Order was soon re-established. The soldiers could not remain deaf to the voice of honor, and those few from whom suffering drew some murmurs unworthy of their courage were soon to redeem themselves by a glorious death.

The following day, the 15th, was the day of an engagement in which my regiment found itself all alone. The Second Division was given the order that morning to abandon the suburb on the right bank, pass through the city, and take up positions on the Vilna road, thus leaving the First Division on the front line to defend the bridgehead. The Fourth Regiment, which occupied the entrance to the suburb, was the most distant from the point of assembly; the calling in of the posts took some time, and General Razout, who was in a hurry to execute the order he had received, began the march without waiting for me. I was leaving as quickly as I could to rejoin the division when the enemy, finding the advance posts deserted, penetrated into the suburb; the stragglers whom they pursued came and took refuge in our ranks. I hastened the march, and when we reached the bridgehead I found the passage so obstructed by the vehicles hastening there that I could not get a single man across. Thus we had to wait, while the press grew greater each moment. The Russians set up two cannon on the height and began to fire on the wagons and my regiment. Now confusion reached its zenith: the drivers jumped from their bullet-riddled vehicles, the Russian infantry and Cossacks advanced. The situation became extremely grave. At all costs we had to repel the attack that might make the enemy master of the bridgehead; but since I was now alone in the suburb, I did not dare engage the enemy when I had received the order to retire. Fortunately Marshal Ney, who was always drawn by cannon fire, appeared on the parapet and ordered me to march against the enemy and drive him from the suburb, and thus gain time to clear the obstacles. I led my regiment out at a charge through the snow and the ruins of houses. The soldiers, proud to fight under the eyes of the Marshal, and of the regiments of the First Division who watched them from the ramparts, threw themselves upon the enemy with the greatest zeal. The Russians withdrew hastily, taking their artillery. We drove their snipers from the houses. In a few moments we were masters of the entire suburb. Marshal Ney then sent me word not to advance too far, an order that seldom came from him. I formed my regiment behind the Petersburg gate, and a very lively fight broke out here with the Russians who had occupied the cemetery of a nearby church, and who were now afraid to come out. This engagement lasted

Fighting in the suburbs

for some time, although the Russians had the advantage in position, numbers and artillery. It was only after receiving the order to return that I began my retreat. It was carried out in good order, and I brought my regiment back to the bridgehead. All the officers had vied with one another in zeal on this occasion; none of them were wounded, and I lost only a few soldiers. The sergeant whom I had broken at the beginning of the retreat, and to whom I had just restored his rank that same morning, was struck at my side by a ball that was perhaps intended for me: he fell dead at my feet.

While the First Division in its turn defended the city, the Second spent the day cleaning its arms and taking a little rest. A detachment of two hundred men from France joined us at Smolensk; I passed them in review and incorporated them into my regiment, which thanks to this reinforcement now numbered over five hundred men. I saw with sorrow how much the exhaustion of the march and the harshness of the season had affected the young men of this detachment. The baggage, which had long marched ahead of us, was also waiting for us at Smolensk. I ordered that it follow us; other colonels sent theirs on ahead, and some of it was saved.

That same evening I received the most complimentary indications of Marshal Ney's satisfaction over our affair of the preceding day; I shared these compliments with the officers, and urged them always to be worthy of them. I thought with pleasure that their task would soon be over, for the Emperor would certainly seize the first opportunity to replace us at the rear guard with fresh troops. There was not an officer who had not been dangerously wounded; five hundred soldiers remained, and how much this group of men had endured! Who would not be inspired by these brave soldiers who, amid so many rude tests, had remained faithful to their flag, and whose courage seemed to grow with privation and dangers! I was proud of the glory which they had acquired. I rejoiced in anticipation of the repose which I hoped they would soon enjoy. This illusion was promptly shattered; but I still like to recall it, and it was the last pleasant thought I experienced during the course of this campaign.

Many wounded and sick officers remained in the hospital at Smolensk. I learned that among them there was an officer of my regiment who had had his hip shot away; I immediately sent after him in order to take him with us. His companions in misfortune remained exposed to the dangers of fire, collapsing walls, and the vengeance of the Russians. The next day the Third Corps was to leave this frightful spot, after having blown up the walls and a large number of caissons which the army could not carry off. Already this city was nothing but a mass of ruins. The windows and doors of the houses which still stood were broken, and the rooms filled with bodies; in the streets were seen the carcasses of horses whose flesh had been devoured by the soldiers and by the inhabitants who had joined them in a common misery. Above all I shall never forget the impression of sadness I felt that night in the deserted streets, lighted by the fires reflected in the snow, and contrasting strangely with the gentle light of the moon. A few years before I had seen this city in all the brilliance of its opulence, and this memory made even more tragic the spectacle of its destruction. The next day, as we were preparing to march, several heavy detonations told us that Smolensk had ceased to exist.

We marched peacefully on the road to Orsha. Cannon could be heard in the distance, and we thought that it was the Ninth Corps which was drawing near to the highway. How could we imagine that the enemy stood

Departure of the Third Corps

in the road before us, without our having been warned by the corps which preceded us? Nevertheless, it was only too certain that the Russian army, by a flanking march, had reached Krasnii while the French were still at Smolensk, and that they were preparing to bar our way. The Emperor, with the Guard, the Fourth, and finally the First Corps, were attacked at Krasnii on the 15th, 16th, and 17th successively. In addition to their superiority of numbers, one can well imagine what advantages the Russians had over tired troops almost without cavalry and artillery. Even so, valor overcame all obstacles; the Imperial Guard, having forced the passage, remained near Krasnii to aid the Fourth and First Corps. The Viceroy and Marshal Davout rejected indignantly the proposals for capitulation which were sent them. They in turn pierced the enemy line, but in doing so lost nearly all their artillery, their baggage, and a large number of prisoners.

The Emperor, who had not a moment to lose in reaching the Beresina, was obliged to abandon the Third Corps and hasten his march toward Orsha. For the three days this affair lasted Marshal Ney received no word of the danger that awaited him in his turn.

The Emperor much critized Marshal Davout for not stopping a day at Krasnii to wait for the Third Corps. The Marshal was sure that he could not have done this; at the very least he should have informed Marshal Ney. Perhaps too, the communication had been intercepted. Be that as it may, General Miloradovich was content to send some light troops in pursuit of the Emperor, and he gathered all his forces against the Third Corps, which he planned to take in its entirety.

On the morning of the 18th we left Korytnia and marched toward Krasnii. The Second Division, which led the march, was harassed by several squadrons of Cossacks as it approached the town. This appearance of the Cossacks meant nothing; we were used to it, and a few musket shots sufficed to drive them off. But soon the advance guard encountered the division of General Richard, which had remained behind, and had just been routed. The Marshal rallied the remains of this division, and thanks to a mist that favored our march and concealed our meager numbers, he approached the enemy until the cannon forced him to stop. The Russian army arrayed in order of battle barred our path: only then did we learn that we had been cut off from the rest of the army, and that our only hope lay in our desperation.

CHAPTER FIVE

Route to Krasnii

Daring plans of Marshal Ney

Passage of the Dnieper

March on the right bank

Critical state of the regiment

Arrival at Orsha

THE BATTLE OF THE THIRD CORPS at Krasnii is one of the finest that distinguished this campaign. Never was a struggle more unequal; never was the skill of the general and the devotion of the troops demonstrated more brilliantly. Marshal Ney had no sooner sheltered his advance guard from the artillery fire than an officer sent by General Miloradovich summoned him to lay down his arms. Those who knew him can understand with what disdain the proposal was received, but the envoy assured him that the high esteem in which the Russian general held his talents and courage would insure that nothing unworthy was proposed. The envoy went on to say that the capitulation was necessary, that the other army corps had abandoned him, that he was facing an army of 80,000 men, and if he wished he could send an officer to confirm this. The Third Corps, with the reinforcements received at Smolensk, did not number 6,000 combatants; the artillery was reduced to six pieces, and the cavalry to a single squad. Even so, the Marshal's only answer was to declare the envoy a prisoner; a few cannon shots fired during this negotiation served as a pretext, and without thinking of the masses of the enemy or his own meager numbers, he ordered the attack.

The Second Division, formed in columns by regiments, marched straight toward the enemy. The Russians watched in admiration as we advanced in the best order and with measured step. Each cannon shot destroyed entire files; each step made death more inevitable, but the pace did not once slacken. Finally we approached so close to the enemy line that the first division of my regiment, completely decimated by the fire, was hurled back upon those who followed, creating great disorder. Then the Russian infantry charged us in its turn, and the cavalry, falling upon our flanks, routed us completely. A few well-placed riflemen stopped the enemy's pursuit for a moment. The Ledru Division was sent into the battle, and our six cannon replied to the fire of the numerous Russian artillery. During this time I rallied what was left of my regiment on the road, where the balls were still striking us. Our attack had not lasted a quarter hour, but the Second Division no longer existed; my regiment lost several officers and was reduced to two hundred men. The Illyrian Regiment and the Eighteenth, which lost its eagle, were even more rudely handled. General Razout was wounded, and General Lenchantin taken prisoner.

Immediately the Marshal withdrew the Second Division toward Smolensk; after a half league he took it to the left across a field, perpendicularly to the road. The First Division, which had long used up its strength sustaining the shock of the whole Russian army, followed this movement with the cannon and some baggage; all the wounded who could walk followed after. The Russians camped in the villages and sent a column of cavalry to observe us.

The day was ending; the Third Corps marched in silence. None of us had any idea of what was going to happen to us. But the presence of Marshal Ney was enough to reassure us. Without knowing what he intended or what he could do, we knew that he would do something. His self-confidence was the equal of his courage. The greater the danger became, the more prompt was his determination; and when he had made up his mind he never doubted success. Thus, in such a moment as this, his face showed neither indecision nor concern; all eyes looked to him, but none dared question him. Finally, seeing an officer of his staff nearby, he said to him in a low voice: "We are in a bad way."

"What are you going to do?" asked the officer.

"Cross the Dnieper."

"Where is the road?"

"We will find it."

"And if it isn't passable?"

"It will be."

"Very well," said the officer.

This singular dialogue, which I quote verbatim, revealed the Marshal's plan to reach Orsha along the right bank of the river, and quickly enough to rejoin the army which was moving along the left bank. The plan was bold and shrewdly conceived; we will see how vigorously it was executed.

We marched across fields without a guide, and the inaccuracy of the maps added to our confusion. Marshal Ney, who had that talent of the military which leads him to seize the least opportunity, noticed some ice in the direction we were moving, and had it broken, thinking that it might be a stream that could lead us to the Dnieper. It was in fact a stream; we followed it and arrived at a village[1] where the Marshal pretended to establish himself. We lit great fires and sent out pickets. The enemy

---

1 Danikova.

Part Two, Chapter Five

left us alone, thinking to make short work of us the next day. Thanks to this strategem the Marshal could continue his plan. We needed a guide but the village was deserted. Finally the soldiers found a lame peasant; they asked him how far it was to the Dnieper and if it were frozen. He replied that the village of Sirokovich was a league away, and here the Dnieper should be frozen. We departed, led by this peasant, and soon we reached the village. The Dnieper was in fact sufficiently frozen to be crossed on foot. While we looked for a place to cross, the houses became filled with wounded officers and men who had managed to drag themselves this far, and for whom the surgeons could scarcely provide the most elementary care; those who were not wounded sought food. Marshal Ney, forgetting the dangers of that day and the day to come, enjoyed a profound sleep.

Towards midnight we took up arms to cross the Dnieper, leaving to the enemy the artillery, the baggage, the wagons, the vehicles of all sorts, and the wounded who could not walk. M. de Briqueville,[2] who had been severely wounded the day before, crossed the Dnieper on his hands and knees; I gave him into the care of the sappers who were able to save him. The ice was so thin that only a small number of horses could cross. The troops reformed on the other side of the river.

Already the first part of Marshal Ney's plan had been achieved; we had crossed the Dnieper, but we were still more than fifteen leagues from Orsha. We had to reach it before the French army departed; what is more, we had to cross unknown territory and resist the enemy's attacks with a handful of exhausted foot soldiers, and without cavalry or artillery. The march began with a good omen: we found Cossacks asleep in a village[3] and

2 Aide-de-camp of the Duke of Placence.
3 Gusinoye.

March on the right bank

made prisoners of them. On the 19th the first rays of the sun found us on the road to Liubovichi. We were stopped only briefly by the fording of a stream and by a few outposts of Cossacks who withdrew at our approach. At noon we had reached two villages situated on a height; their inhabitants had barely time to run off, abandoning their food to us. The soldiers were rejoicing in this abundance when we heard the cry "To arms!" The enemy was advancing and had just driven in our pickets. The troops left the villages, reformed in columns, and resumed their march in the presence of the enemy. But these latter were no longer the few Cossacks such as we had encountered before: they were now whole squadrons maneuvering in order and commanded by General Platov himself. Our fire held them back and the columns hastened their step while preparing themselves for an attack of the cavalry. Numerous as this cavalry was, we did not really fear it, for the Cossacks never dared a serious charge against a square of infantry; but soon several cannon opened fire on our columns. This artillery was following the movement of the cavalry, and was being moved by sledges wherever it would act with effect. Until nightfall Marshal Ney continued to struggle against all these obstacles, making use of every advantage in the terrain. Amid all the shells which fell in our ranks and despite the cries and feints of the Cossacks, we marched along steadily. Night was approaching, and the enemy redoubled his efforts. We had to leave the road and turn to the left into the woods which bordered the Dnieper. The Cossacks had already occupied these woods, and the Fourth and Eighteenth, led by General d'Hénin, were charged with driving them out. Meanwhile the enemy artillery had taken up position on the far side of a ravine through which we had to pass. It was here that General Platov planned to exterminate us all.

Part Two, Chapter Five

I followed my regiment into the woods. The Cossacks drew back, but the woods were deep and tangled, and we had to look in all directions in order to prevent a surprise. Night came, and we no longer heard a sound. It was more than likely that Marshal Ney had continued to advance. I advised General d'Hénin to follow his movement; he refused, fearing the Marshal's reprimand if he left without orders the place where he had been posted. Just then loud cries which heralded a charge were heard in front of us and at some distance; thus it was certain that our column had continued its march, and we were going to be cut off. I redoubled my pleas to General d'Hénin, assuring him that I knew the Marshal's way of doing things, and that he would send no order, relying on each commander to act according to the circumstances; moreover, he was now too far away to communicate with us, and the Eighteenth had surely left some time ago. The General persisted in his refusal; all I could obtain from him was that he would lead us to where the Eighteenth was supposed to have been, so as to unite the two regiments. The Eighteenth was gone, and we found in its place a squadron of Cossacks. General d'Hénin, convinced too late of the correctness of my observations, now desired to rejoin the column. But we had moved through the woods in so many directions that we no longer knew which way to go; the fires that we could see here and there only confused us more. We consulted the officers of my regiment and followed the direction that the greater number of them indicated.

I will not attempt to describe all that we had to suffer during that cruel night. I had not more than a hundred men, and we were more than a league behind our column. We had to rejoin it in the midst of enemies who surrounded us. We had to march rapidly enough to make up the lost time, and in sufficiently good order to repel the attacks of the Cossacks. The darkness of the night, our uncertainty over the path we were taking, the difficulty of marching through woods—all this increased our difficulties. The Cossacks shouted to us to surrender and fired directly into our midst; those who were struck were left behind. A sergeant had his leg shattered by a rifle shot. He fell beside me, saying calmly to his comrades: "I am finished; take my knapsack, you can use it." They took the knapsack, and we left him in silence. Two wounded officers suffered the same fate. But I noticed with some alarm the attitude which this situation was producing on the soldiers, and even on the officers of my regiment. He who had been a hero on the battlefield was now nervous and alarmed; so true is it that the circumstances of danger frighten more than the danger itself. A very small number kept the presence of mind that was so necessary to us. I needed all my authority to maintain order in the march, and to keep anyone from leaving the ranks. An officer even dared suggest that we might be forced to surrender. I reprimanded him aloud, and all the more severely because he was an officer of merit: this made the lesson more telling.

Finally after an hour we left the woods and found the Dnieper on our left. We were thus going in the right direction, and this discovery gave the soldiers a moment of joy; I took advantage of it to encourage them and to urge them to retain the sangfroid which alone could save us. General d'Hénin led us along the river to prevent the enemy from turning us. We were far from being out of danger: we had no more doubts about our direction, but the plain along which we were marching permitted the enemy to attack us in mass and use his artillery. Fortunately it was dark and the artillery fired at random. From time to time the Cossacks approached with loud cries: we halted to repulse them with a volley and marched on again immediately. This march took us two leagues over very difficult terrain. We crossed ravines so steep that we could hardly clamber up the opposite side, and we forded half-frozen streams in water up to our knees. Nothing shook the constancy of the soldiers: we always kept the best order, and none left the ranks. General d'Hénin, who had been wounded by a shell fragment, said nothing about it so as not to discourage the soldiers; he continued to command us with the same energy. He might well be reproached for having lingered too long in his defense of the woods at the Dnieper, but in such difficult times error must be pardoned. What is more, none can deny that he led us with courage and ability during that perilous march. The enemy's pursuit at last slackened; on a height before us we discovered some camp fires. It was Marshal Ney's rear guard, which had halted there and was about to resume its march; we rejoined it and learned that the previous day Marshal Ney had marched on the enemy artillery and forced a passage.

It was thus that the Fourth Regiment extricated itself from a position that was well-nigh hopeless. The march lasted another hour. The soldiers were exhausted, and we stopped in a village where there were a few provisions.

We were still eight leagues from Orsha, and General Platov would no doubt redouble his efforts to overcome us. Time was precious; at one o'clock in the morning the drums beat assembly and we departed. The village was in flames; the darkness of the night, lit only by the fire, cast strange shadows about us. I watched this spectacle with much sadness. The exhaustion of the preceding day and the water still in my boots made my suffering surpass anything I had endured before. Scarce able to walk, I leaned on the arm of M. Lalande, a young officer of the *voltigeurs*. His conduct at the beginning of the campaign had brought him several reprimands, and he had been denied the rank of captain, to which his seniority as a lieutenant entitled him. I observed him carefully, and since I was very pleased with him, I thought it time to promise him some compensation. I thus told him of my satisfaction and of my regrets over the delay in his advancement, giving him my word that he would be the next captain appointed in my regiment. He thanked me with much feeling, and redoubled his devotion so long as his strength was equal to his courage. This unfortunate young man was to die in the end; but I like to think that the hope which I gave him sustained his courage for a time, and mitigated the horror of his last moments.

We marched until daybreak without being disturbed. At the first rays of the sun the Cossacks reappeared, and soon the road which we followed led us into a plain. General Platov, who hoped to take advantage of this brought forward that artillery on sledges which we could neither avoid nor attain; and when he thought that he had brought sufficient disorder in our ranks, he ordered a charge in earnest. Marshal Ney quickly formed each of his two divisions into a square; the Second, commanded by General d'Hénin, was in the rear guard and the first to be attacked. We forced into our ranks all the stragglers who still carried muskets; we had to use the direst threats to make them serve. The Cossacks, who were but feebly resisted by our skirmishers, drove before them a great crowd of stragglers without arms as they attempted to reach our square. The soldiers hastened their march at the approach of the enemy and under the fire of his artillery. Twenty times I saw them on the point of disbanding and scattering, delivering us all up to the mercies of the Cossacks; but the presence of Marshal Ney, the confidence he inspired, and his calm manner in such time of danger held them to their duty. We reached the top of a rise. The Marshal ordered General d'Hénin to hold there, adding that he should be ready to die there for the honor of France. Meanwhile General Ledru marched on Yokubov,[4] a village bordering a wood. When he was established there we rejoined him; the two divisions took up positions flanking each other. It was not yet noon, but Marshal Ney declared that he would defend this village until nine o'clock in the evening. General Platov tried countless times to carry it; his attacks were consistently beaten back, and discouraged at so much resistance, he took up a position opposite us.

That morning the Marshal had dispatched a Polish officer who managed to reach Orsha and deliver news of us. The Emperor had left the day before; the Viceroy and Marshal Davout still occupied the town.

At nine in the evening we shouldered arms and resumed our march in the greatest silence. The outposts of Cossacks placed on the road before us retired at our approach. The march continued in good order. At a league from Orsha the advance guard challenged an outpost. They were answered in French. It was a division of the Fourth Corps coming to our aid with the Viceroy. One would have had to spend three days between life and death in order to appreciate the joy which this encounter brought us. The Viceroy received us with the greatest emotion. He told Marshal Ney publicly of his admiration for his conduct. He complimented the generals and the two colonels who remained.[5] His aides-de-camp surrounded us, overwhelming us with questions on the details of this great drama and on the part each of us had played in it. But time pressed: after a few minutes we had once again to start for Orsha. The Viceroy insisted on taking over the rear guard. At three o'clock in the morning

[4] So called in the report of Platov. It should be Teolino.
[5] Colonel Pelleport of the 18th and myself.

Arrival at Orsha

we entered the town. A few miserable houses in the suburb sufficed us for shelter. We were promised a distribution of food in the morning, and at last we could take a little rest.

Thus ended this audacious march, one of the strangest episodes of the campaign. In it Marshal Ney covered himself with glory. To him the Third Corps owed its salvation, if indeed one could call an army corps the eight or nine hundred men who reached Orsha, all that remained of the 6,000 men who had fought at Krasnii.

CHAPTER SIX

Movements of the other corps

Disorganization of the army

March to Veselovo

Movements of the Russian armies

Reunion of the grand army

Passage of the Beresina

Affair of 28 November

WHILE THE THIRD CORPS endured the terrible struggle that I have just related, the Emperor had marched rapidly to Orsha, continually pursued by the light troops of the Russians. The details of this movement offer nothing of interest save the tragic death of three hundred men of the First Corps, burned alive at Lyadi in a barn in which they were spending the night. These unfortunates so struggled with one another in their attempts to save themselves that none of them got out. All of them perished; a sole survivor was still breathing, and he had to be shot twice to end his agony.

I explained at the end of the third chapter the situation of the army, and how necessary it was to cross the Beresina before the Russians; thus Napoleon did not stop at Orsha, but continued down the road to Borisov. This latter town is on the Beresina at some thirty leagues' distance from Orsha; the Dombrowski Division had been established there to guard the bridge.

Now a new era began for the Third Corps. We have seen that this corps alone was charged with the rear guard from Vyazma; that

Disorganization of the army

is for an interval of eighteen days and a distance of sixty leagues. Now reunited with the main army and marching in its ranks we were to partake only of the common fatigues and privations.

We had scarcely had three hours of repose at Orsha when we began to think of the distribution of provisions; but we were even to be deprived of this feeble resource. The Russians, who were on the other side of the Dnieper, had begun to set fire to the town with their shells. The buildings containing the provisions were easily visible and served as aiming points. It became impossible to make any regular distributions; some soldiers brought out brandy and flour at the risk of their lives. Marshal Davout, now charged with the rear guard, hastened our departure.

At eight o'clock in the morning we were on the road to Borisov. This road is one of the finest to be seen anywhere, and its width permitted several columns to march side by side. For the first time I did not have to think of the enemy, and I examined the state of my regiment; I had barely eighty men left, and how could I hope to preserve this small number of soldiers when I could not give them an instant of repose? I noticed with anguish the wretched condition of their uniforms and their shoes, their emaciation, and the haggard expression on their faces. The other regiments of the Third Corps were perhaps even in worse state than mine. The lack of food in itself would have sufficed to destroy the army had it not been joined to all the other calamities. Long ago the provisions from Moscow had been exhausted, the wagons which carried them abandoned, and the horses dead along the roads. We have already seen what portion of the distributions fell our lot, and these, moreover, had only taken place in Smolensk and Orsha. As for the resources in the countryside, one can well imagine what remained in those areas that had been traversed by troops preceding us. Thus we lived in a manner that was almost miraculous, sometimes with flour mixed in water and without salt, sometimes with a little honey or a few morsels of horsemeat, and with no other drink than melted snow. As we approached Vilna, we obtained a kind of drink made from beets. The cold had much diminished; it will be recalled that we found the Dnieper barely frozen. Yet this change in temperature was of no advantage to us. The partial thaw only made the ground more slippery, wore out shoes, and increased our exhaustion. At some distance from Orsha I encountered M. Lanusse, a captain in my regiment who had been blinded by a gunshot wound at the taking of Smolensk; a *cantinière* from his company was leading him and caring for him. He told me that after being captured and robbed by the Cossacks at Krasnii, they had managed to get away and they were going to try to follow us. A short time later they were found on the road, dead and stripped of their clothes.

The other army corps which marched with us had lost fewer men than we; but their misery was as great, and their disorganization as complete. In this respect the Guard was no different from the rest of the army. The cavalry had ceased to exist long ago. Napoleon collected all the officers who still had horses to form a sort of mounted guard around himself; generals served as officers and colonels as non-commissioned officers. This body, which he himself called the "Holy Squadron," was under the direct orders of the King of Naples; but the calamities of the retreat prevented any use of it. It was disbanded soon after its formation.

In five days' march the army reached the Beresina. We came upon headquarters at Tolochin. The Emperor congratulated Marshal Ney on his expedition at the Dnieper; then he talked to him, with great calm, about the dangers which awaited the army at the passage of the

March to Veselovo

Beresina, and he did not minimize their extent. We spent two nights sheltered in the little towns of Bobr and Nacha. I cannot say the same for Nemants, situated a league from Borisov; the nearness of the Beresina caused a great congestion, and the soldiers of all the army corps became mixed pell-mell with the wounded. A general, whose name I forget, had taken lodgings in a fine house. The major of my regiment took it into his head to ask him to extend hospitality to us; he refused, which was unpardonable, and the major, very overwrought, got so angry that he threatened to set fire to the house—to such an extent had indiscipline spread at this time! I gave the major a stern reprimand, and after having apologized to the general in his name, I spent the night with officers of my regiment inside the walls of a hut which had lost its roof. Before relating the crossing of the Beresina, I must say a word about the general situation of the army and that of the enemy.

We have seen, at the end of chapter three, that General Wittgenstein had taken Polotsk on October 18, and that the Second Corps, driven from its position on the Dnieper, had moved toward the road which we were following. As soon as the Duke of Bellune[1] had arrived with the Ninth and had relieved the Second, the Duke of Reggio came and took up a position at Bobr. The Duke of Bellune, after an indecisive engagement at Chashniki, on the 11th of November, had held General Wittgenstein until the 22nd, and then had begun a retrograde movement so as to draw nearer to the main army.

Elsewhere, Admiral Chichagov, coming from Moldavia, had surprised the town of Minsk on November 16, and had seized all the stores there. His advance guard had seized the bridge at Borisov on the 21st, despite the des-

---

1 Claude-Victor Perrin, created Duke of Bellune in 1808. [Ed.]

perate resistance of General Dombrowski, had crossed the Beresina and moved in front of the Emperor on the road from Orsha. The Duke of Reggio had marched to meet the Russians, and had driven them back to Borisov and across the Beresina, after which they had burned the bridge. Finally, the commanding general, Kutusov, who had been following us since Moscow with the main army, had continued his movement on our left flank and had combined his operations with those of the other corps. Thus three Russian armies were preparing to encircle the French army on the banks of the Beresina: the army from Moldavia, on the far bank, barring the passage; the corps of General Wittgenstein, pressing the rear guard on the right and driving it toward the center; the main army, carrying out the same maneuver on the left. To these formidable attacks must be added the impossiblity of feeding the French troops united in such a small space, the necessity of building a bridge over the Beresina under the eyes of the enemy, and finally the fatigue and exhaustion of our army. On the other hand, the reincorporation of the Second and Ninth Corps, the latter almost intact, and the former much better preserved than our own, would be of great help to us; we still had 50,000 combatants, 5,000 horsemen, a sizeable artillery, the genius of the Emperor, and the courage that is born of despair. Moreover, the slowness of pursuit of the main Russian army kept it out of the battle line, since General Kutusov only crossed the Dnieper at Kopys on the 26th of November, while the entire French army stood united on the banks of the Beresina on the 25th, three days' march ahead. Thus we had to cross the Beresina sufficiently quickly to avoid being attacked by General Kutusov, and consequently have only two armies to fight instead of three. The Second Corps, placed at Borisov, was to attempt the crossing; the Ninth was to delay the march of General Wittgenstein on the left bank. The other corps, too worn out to be of any use, were ordered to march between the Second and the Ninth. The Imperial Guard was kept as our last resource.

As early as the 24th the Emperor was occupied with finding a place to cross. We could not make the attempt at Borisov itself, for we would have to build a bridge and cross it under the fire of the enemy batteries on the opposite bank. Below Borisov, at Ukholody, we would be closer to General Kutusov, whom it was so necessary to avoid. By contrast, three leagues above Borisov at the village of Veselovo, the terrain favored us: the heights on our side dominated the other shore, and the passage could be attempted here; moreover, on the other side was the Zembin road, by which the army could be taken back to Vilna. Napoleon chose this last place. The day of the 25th was spent in making feints to cross at Ukholody and above all at Borisov. Admiral Chichagov, who had only 20,000 infantry in all, could not occupy in force all the crossing points; he directed his principal concern on Borisov and on the points below this town, where General Kutusov assured him the French army would head. Meanwhile, on the night of the 25th to the 26th, the Second Corps moved to Veselovo; the Emperor arrived there at dawn on the 26th. Some horsemen with skirmishers mounted behind them swam the river and attacked the Russian pickets. Immediately thirty cannon were placed on the heights which dominated the opposite bank to prevent the enemy from massing there. Under the protection of this artillery the engineers worked in the ice-filled water to build two bridges which they finished before nightfall. The Second Corps crossed and drove the Russians back along the road to Borisov; the other army corps followed. The Third Corps arrived at Veselovo in the evening and crossed the Beresina a little before daybreak. Many men stayed on the left bank, thinking it would be easier to cross the following morning; others scattered into the half-frozen marshes along the right bank, searching in vain for shelter against the bitter cold.

At dawn the Third Corps reformed and took position behind the Second in a wood traversed by the road. The day passed calmly. Chichagov, apprised of the passage of our army, assembled his forces to attack us, while the First, Fourth, and Fifth Corps, the Emperor and the Imperial Guard, the artillery parks and the baggage passed continuously over the bridges, which kept breaking at every turn. At first the passage was conducted with a fair degree of order; but the crowd grew steadily, and the confusion became such that the troops had to use force in order to get through.

The cold had returned: the snow fell heavily, and the fires we built could scarcely keep us warm. I was nevertheless determined to put this day to good use. Since Smolensk I had not had the time or courage to examine closely the destruction of my regiment. That day I decided to take up those grim details. I summoned my officers and called the roll from the list I had brought from Moscow: how many changes since then! Of seventy officers there remained scarcely forty, and most of these were sick or overcome with exhaustion. I talked to them for a long time about our situation. To several I gave the praises that their truly heroic conduct merited; I reproached others of them who had shown weakness, and promised them that I would always try to encourage them by my example. Nearly all the company officers had been lost at Krasnii, and this made discipline all the more difficult. I formed two squads from the soldiers who remained, one composed of grenadiers and *voltigeurs* and the other of companies of the line. I appointed officers to command them, ordering the others to get a musket and march with me at the head of the regiment. As for myself I was at the end of my resources. I had only one horse left; my last valise was lost in the passage of the Beresina, and all that remained was what I carried on my person; and we were still fifty leagues from Vilna and eighty from the Niemen. But I took little heed of my personal sufferings in the midst of so much misfortune. Marshal Ney had lost everything, as we had, and his aides-de-camp were dying of hunger. I still recall with gratitude that more than once they were kind enough to share with me the little food they could find.

That same evening a tragic event befell the Ninth Corps on the right bank. The Duke of Bellune had arrived at Borisov on the 26th, still followed by General Wittgenstein. On the 27th he came to Veselovo to protect the passage and use it himself. The Partonneaux Divison, serving as rear guard, was left at Borisov, with orders to rejoin the main body that night. The General, who had no guide and was apparently confused by the campfires of the enemy, took the wrong road. He marched into the middle of General Wittgenstein's troops and was taken with his entire division, 4,000 men strong. Wittgenstein, having no obstacle before him, marched rapidly on Veselovo.

The next day, the 28th, a lively combat took place on both sides of the river. Admiral Chichagov on the left bank and General Wittgenstein on the right made a joint effort to drive our troops back and throw them into the Beresina. Against the Admiral's attacks we could only oppose the Second Corps and a part of the Fifth. Three feeble battalions placed on the high road were the reserve; these were all that remained of the First, Third, and Eighth Corps. The struggle had lasted for some time when the Second Corps, sorely pressed by superior forces, began to give way. Our reserve, which came under fire, moved to the rear. This movement caused all the isolated soldiers who filled the woods to take flight, and in their panic they ran all the way to the bridge. Even the Young Guard was shaken. Soon there was no hope save the Old Guard; we stood ready to conquer or perish alongside them. In an instant the picture changed completely, and the place that was to be the tomb of the Grand Army was the site of its last triumph. The Duke of Reggio had just been wounded after a heroic resistance; Marshal Ney replaced him immediately. That famous warrior, who had saved the Third Corps at Krasnii, now saved the entire army and the Emperor himself on the banks of the Beresina. He rallied the Second Corps and boldly resumed the offensive. His experience guided the generals just as his courage animated the soldiers. The Doumerc Cuirassiers shattered the Russian squares and carried off the cannon. The French and Polish infantry seconded these efforts; 4,000 prisoners and five cannon were the fruits of this victory. We joyfully acclaimed the brave soldiers who brought us these trophies. Their valor decided the day. Chichagov, who had not expected to find his enemy so redoubtable, did not renew the attack. Night came: the Second Corps kept its position and the others reentered the woods and returned to their camps. The night was as severe as the preceding ones; but it was not we who were to be pitied, but those unfortunates who remained on the other shore.

Disorder had steadily increased on the day and night of the 27th. On the morning of the 28th the bridge for the vehicles disintegrated completely; the artillery and baggage moved to the other bridge destined for the infantry and forcibly opened a passage for themselves. On that side of the river there were only the two divisions of the Ninth Corps; but there were also huge numbers of wagons and vehicles of all sorts; stragglers and noncombatants, among whom there were many women and children. Express orders were given that the troops were to cross first; the vehicles and the wounded, sick and others that the army dragged in its wake were to cross afterward, protected by the Ninth Corps, which was to bring up the rear. But General Wittgenstein, who had already captured the entire Partonneaux Division as we have seen, attacked the Duke of Bellune on the morning of the 28th near Veselovo, and thus renewed on his side the same effort that the Admiral was making on the other bank. The Duke of Bellune used all his skill and bravery in the defense; but pressed by superior numbers, he could not check the enemy's progress. Towards evening the Russian artillery took a favorable position and began firing into the confused mass which covered the plain. The disorder was then at its worst; horses and vehicles rode over the bodies of those whom they struck down. Each thought only of saving himself, and to clear a passage he did not hesitate to strike down his neighbor or throw him into the stream. In the middle of this confusion the cannon balls struck those still on the bridge, and demolished the wagons; a great many men died on the bridge; others tried to swim across and were drowned in the ice-filled water. It was dark and the Ninth Corps still fought. Soon the Duke of Bellune withdrew his troops, made it to the bridge, crossed it rapidly, and then set it afire. The dead and dying who still littered it were swallowed up by the waters, and all those on the other side fell into the hands of the enemy, along with the baggage, much artillery, private vehicles, the plunder from Moscow; indeed, all that had survived the previous disasters. More than 15,000 men were killed or made prisoner on that terrible day.

CHAPTER SEVEN

First days of march

Difficulties with the rear guard

Movements of the Third Corps

Departure of the Emperor

Renewed intensity of the cold

Arrival of the army at Vilna

WE HAD CROSSED THE BERESINA, and the Russian plan had failed; but the pitiable condition of the army made it more and more difficult to resist new attacks. The Second and Ninth Corps, which had sacrificed themselves to open the Beresina to us, were now in as bad a state as we were, and the salvation of the army depended upon the rapidity of its flight. Thus this part of the retreat, the most disastrous of all, offers only the spectacle of a hasty march, or rather of a long rout without any military operations. We hoped to rally our army at Vilna under the protection of some fresh troops there. We were still some forty leagues away on the Zembin road, which joined the highway at Molodechno; we headed in that direction.

On the 28th, when Chichagov's attack had been repulsed, Napoleon moved to Zembin with the Guard and the First, Fourth, and Fifth Corps. On the morning of the 29th the Second and Ninth began their retreat, followed by the Third. The Zembin road is a wooden one built above the marshes, as are several others in this region; some very long bridges traverse the streams that empty into the Beresina. This disposition of the terrain made the march slow and difficult; since the marshes were but half frozen, the entire column had to move along the road, which was often very narrow; but we consoled ourselves with the thought that had the enemy been less concerned with defending the road to Minsk and more attentive to the route to Vilna, he need only have burned one of the bridges to drive us into the marshes. After having crossed one of these bridges, the Third Corps halted for a time to regroup. There I watched the pell-mell passage of officers of all ranks, soldiers, servants, a few horsemen leading their mounts with difficulty, and the lame and wounded helping one another along. Each of them told some miraculous way in which he had escaped the disaster at the Beresina, and congratulated himself that he had saved his life by abandoning all he possessed. I noticed an Italian officer who was barely breathing, carried by two soldiers and accompanied by his wife. Deeply touched by the misfortune of this woman and her concern for her husband, I gave her my place before the fire we had built. Her husband expired, but she continued to call him until she could no longer doubt her loss, and then she fell unconscious upon his body. Such were the sad spectacles which we beheld when we stopped momentarily, along with the quarrels of the soldiers who fought over a piece of horsemeat or a little flour; for some time now the only means of preserving one's life was to take by force provisions from those who still had them, or to steal them from their owners while they slept.

That same day I learned of the death of M. Alfred de Noailles, aide-de-camp of the Prince of Neuchâtel: he had been killed the day before at the side of the Duke of Reggio. Up to that time I had not lost any of my friends, and I was overcome with sorrow. When I spoke of this to Marshal Ney, all he said to me by way of consolation was that apparently his time had come, and that after all it was better that we should grieve for him than that he should grieve for us. On such occasions he always showed the same lack of feeling; another time I heard him say to a poor wounded man who asked to be carried along: "What do you want me to do? You are a victim of the war"; and he rode on. It was certainly not that he was evil or cruel: long acquaintance with the misfortunes of war had hardened his heart. Convinced that all soldiers should die on the field of battle, he found it quite natural that they should fulfill their destiny; we have already seen in this account that he put no more value on his own life than on the lives of others.

The Third Corps reached Zembin on the 29th and Kamen the 30th. The march had scarcely begun when the Duke of Bellune declared that he could no longer serve as the rear guard. He even tried to pass us and leave the Third Corps exposed to the attacks of the Russian advance guard; this caused heated discussion between him and Marshal Ney. They appealed to the authority of Napoleon, who ordered the Duke of Bellune to stay in the rear and protect the retreat.[1] But this incident made us feel very little confidence in the Ninth Corps; consequently Marshal Ney wanted to remove from danger what remained of the Third Corps, that is, a few officers and the eagles of the regiments. He gathered all the soldiers able to fight under the command of a captain;[2] there were barely a hundred. This body was to serve as escort to the Marshal. All the rest left Kamen at midnight under command of General Ledru. We were to try to rejoin the Emperor so as to march with the Imperial Guard and under its protection. Since headquarters had a day's start on us, we

---

1 December 2.
2 M. Delachau, captain of the Fourth Regiment, later colonel of the Twenty-ninth.

had to hasten all the more with forced marches. Thus for two days and three nights we marched almost continuously, and when the excess of fatigue forced us to take a few moments of rest we gathered in a barn with the eagles and the few armed soldiers who guarded them. Soon we were ordered to break the eagles to pieces and bury them. I could not do it. I had the staff burned and put the eagle in the haversack of one of the eagle bearers, and I always marched beside him.

At the same time the officers were again given the order to arm themselves with muskets. This order was impossible of execution: the officers were ill and weak, and no longer had the strength to use the weapons. Several succumbed during this march; one of them, who had recently married in France, was found dead near a campfire, holding the portrait of his wife tightly pressed against his heart. All of us came very close to being taken by the Cossacks in the little town of Ilia. Luckily a battalion of the Old Guard had remained with Count Lobau to protect the position, and they came to our aid. On the 3rd we rejoined headquarters between Ilia and Molodechno; but this headquarters, which had been so brilliant at the beginning of the campaign, was no longer recognizable. The Guard marched in disorder; sorrow and discontent were written on the faces of the soldiers. The Emperor rode in a carriage with the Prince of Neuchâtel; the small number of draft horses, saddle horses, and mules who had escaped so many disasters followed the carriage. The aides-de-camp of the Emperor and of the Prince of Neuchâtel led their horses, which could barely walk. Sometimes to take a little rest they sat on the back of the carriage. Along with this sad cortege there moved a mass of wounded and lame soldiers, marching without order. The forest of pines through which we passed lent darker shades to this picture, and seemed to increase its horror.

Part Two, Chapter Seven

When we left the forest we found ourselves at Molodechno, a crossroads on the highway from Minsk to Vilna.

It was of the greatest importance that we reach this point before the Russians could seize it and bar our path. The rapidity of our march prevented this misfortune, but the enemy had not ceased harassing us from all directions. From the Beresina their three armies continued to march along three separate routes. Chichagov with the army of Moldavia formed the advance guard and followed the same road that we did; Kutusov marched on our left flank, Wittgenstein on our right.

The Sixth Corps, commanded by General de Wrede, had retired to Dokshitsy after the affair at Polotsk; it continued its movement toward Vilna by way of Vileika and Nememzin. This march covered the army's flank; but the Sixth Corps had been so nearly destroyed that it could be of but little service. The Cossacks charged our column without warning and massacred almost without resistance those whom they reached. At Pleshchenitsy the Duke of Reggio, who had been wounded, was attacked in a wooden house where he had taken shelter. A cannon ball shattered the bed on which he was lying, and a fragment of it gave him a second wound. He owed his survival to a few officers, equally wounded, who held the besieged house until the arrival of the first French troops. At Chotainski and at Molodechno the Ninth Corps, which had the rear guard, was heavily attacked and completely routed. The Duke of Bellune himself declared that this was his last effort, and that considering the state of his troops, he was going to hasten his march and avoid any kind of engagement.[3] Napoleon was unable to do anything further with

---

3 It is difficult to understand the Emperor's illusions. On December 3rd and 4th he indicated in his orders his intention to have the army stay at Molodechno or Smorgon. He spoke of distributing supplies. On the 5th, at the moment of his departure, he was still ordering the King of Naples to keep Vilna, or at least Kovno, as a bridgehead.

an army so completely demolished; moreover he was fearful of the effects which the news of this disaster might produce in Germany. He decided to leave the army and return to France in order to obtain new resources with which to carry on the war. The time was favorable, for the occupation of Molodechno had reopened communications with Vilna. On the 5th of December he wrote in Smorgon the celebrated Twenty-ninth Bulletin,[4] and left that same evening on a sled with the Grand Marshal, the Grand Equerry, and Count Lobau, leaving to the King of Naples the command of the army. This departure was judged variously. Some cried that they had been abandoned; others found solace in the thought that the Emperor would return soon at the head of the new army to avenge us. Many simply said they wished they could go away as he did.

In the situation in which the army found itself, this event was a new calamity. The belief in the Emperor's genius brought confidence; the fear which he inspired kept men at their duty. After his departure each did as he wished, and the orders which the King of Naples issued only compromised his authority. I have said that the cadres of the Third Corps had rejoined the Imperial Guard and marched under its protection. The day after Napoleon's departure the King of Naples sought to send us back to the rear guard. Nevertheless, General Ledru continued his march. The Loison Division, ten thousand strong, and two Neapolitan regiments had come from Vilna to take up a position at Oshmyani and protect the army's retreat. In two days of bivouac, without a single engagement, the cold had reduced them to the same condition as ourselves.

[4] This famous bulletin was written on December 3rd and published in Paris on the 16th. It first revealed to the French people the appalling nature of the disaster. It concluded with the reassuring statement that Napoleon's health had "never been better." [Ed.]

Part Two, Chapter Seven

The bad example of the other regiments completed their disorder; they were swept along in the general rout, and all the debris of the army arrived pell-mell in Vilna.

It would serve no purpose to relate the details of each day's march in this period: that would simply be repeating an account of the same misfortunes. The cold, which had seemed to slacken only in order to make more difficult the crossing of the Dnieper and the Beresina, now became more intense than ever. The thermometer dropped first to 15 and 18 degrees, then to 20 and 25 degrees,[5] and the rigors of the weather completed the destruction of men already half dead from hunger and fatigue. I will not attempt to describe the scenes we beheld. Imagine vast snow-covered plains stretching as far as the eye can see, deep pine forests, half-burned and deserted villages, and marching through this mournful countryside an immense column of miserable wretches, almost all without weapons, moving along rag-tag and bobtail, slipping on the ice at each step and falling down beside the carcasses of horses and the corpses of their comrades. Their faces bore the impress of resignation or despair, their eyes were dead, their features without expression and blackened with dirt and smoke. Sheepskins and strips of cloth served them as shoes; their heads were wrapped in rags, their shoulders covered with horse blankets, women's skirts, or half-cured hides. As soon as one of them fell from exhaustion, his comrades stripped him before he was dead and dressed in his rags. Each camp resembled the morrow of a battle. We found dead beside us those with whom we had lain

---

[5] The figures which Fezensac gives here are most probably degrees below zero in the Réaumur scale, still widely used in the period; they would correspond to temperatures ranging from –3 degrees to –25 degrees Fahrenheit. Actually the cold was often much more severe in late November and early December than Fezensac indicates. Several times the temperature dropped below –40 degrees Fahrenheit. [Ed.]

down the evening before. An officer of the Russian advance guard was a witness to these scenes of horror which the rapidity of our flight gave us but little time to observe; he has drawn a picture to which nothing could be added:

> The road that we travelled was covered with prisoners whom we took no care to guard, and who were in an extremity of suffering previously unknown; many still dragged themselves mechanically along the road on their naked and half-frozen feet; some had lost the power of speech; others had fallen into a kind of savage stupor, and sought despite our efforts to cook the cadavers and devour them. Those too feeble to gather wood stopped near the first fire they found; there, sitting one on the other, they huddled around that fire whose paltry heat sustained them, and the little life remaining in them was extinguished with the flames. The houses and barns to which these wretches had set fire were ringed with their bodies; for those who came close had not the strength to flee the flames which reached them; and sometimes we saw others with a convulsive smile hurl themselves intentionally into the middle of the fire, which consumed them in their turn.[6]

Amid such terrible calamities I watched the destruction of my regiment with the keenest anguish. That was my greatest suffering, or more truthfully, my only one,

[6] The horrible, touching, and often unbelievable anecdotes that could be told of this tragic period are endless:
A general, overcome with exhaustion, had fallen on the road. A soldier passing by started to take his boots. The general roused himself with difficulty and asked the soldier to wait at least until he was dead before he began despoiling him. "My General," replied the soldier, "I would be glad to do so, but then someone else would take your boots, and it might as well be me who gets them," and he continued removing the boots.
A soldier was being stripped by one of his fellows; he asked to be left alone that he might die in peace. "Excuse me, comrade,"

for I do not call by that name such things as hunger, cold, and fatigue. When the body resists physical suffering, our courage soon learns to disdain them, above all when it is sustained by the belief in God and the hope of another life. But I confess that courage abandoned me as I watched the death of the friends and comrades in arms who are so rightly called the colonel's family, which he had seemingly been called to command only in order to preside at their destruction. Nothing brings us closer together than common misfortunes; and I always found in those men the same attachment and concern which they inspired in me. Never did an officer or soldier have a piece of bread without coming to share it with me. This mutual concern was

---

said the other soldier, "I thought you were dead," and he went away.

Sometimes a frightful humor was present along with egoism and cruelty. Two soldiers heard an ill officer lying nearby who called them to help him and told them he was an officer of engineers. "What, you're an officer of engineers?" they asked stopping by him. "Yes, my friends," the officer replied. "Well, draw a map then," said one of the soldiers, and they left him there.

By way of contrast, and to the credit of humanity, some sublime instances of devotion could be found among so much egoism and insensitiveness. Notably there was the case of a drummer in the Seventh Regiment of light infantry. His wife, the *cantinière* of the regiment, fell ill at the beginning of the retreat. The drummer drove her as long as they had a horse and cart. At Smolensk the horse died; then the drummer pulled the cart himself as far as Vilna. When they reached this town the wife was too ill to travel further, and her husband became a prisoner in order to stay with her.

A *cantinière* of the Thirty-Third Regiment had given birth to a daughter in Prussia before the campaign began. The baby followed the regiment to Moscow along with her mother, and was six months old when we left Moscow. This infant survived the retreat in a manner that was truly miraculous. Her mother fed her nothing but horseblood sausage; she was wrapped in a fur picked up in Moscow, and was often bareheaded. Twice she was lost and found again, once in a field and once in a burned village, sleeping on a mattress. Her mother crossed the Beresina on horseback, with water up to her neck, holding the reins in one hand and balancing the child on top of her head with the other. Thus, by a succession of miracles, this little girl survived the retreat without accident, and indeed never even caught a cold.

Arrival of the army at Vilna

not unique in my regiment; it could be found in the entire army, in that army where authority was so paternal and where subordination was almost always based on attachment and confidence. It has been said that at this period one's superiors were ignored and mistreated; at most that could only have occurred among strangers, for within the regiment no colonel ceased to be respected so long as he merited that respect. The only way to alleviate so many sorrows was to march together and aid and comfort one another. In this way we advanced toward Vilna, counting each step that took us closer, sleeping packed in miserable huts close to headquarters, arriving at night, leaving before dawn. A drummer of the Twenty-fourth Regiment marched at our head; he was all that remained of the regimental drummers and musicians of the Third Corps.

On the 8th of December, five days after Napoleon's departure, we arrived under the walls of Vilna.[7] I had gone ahead that day with General Ledru's permission, in order to learn what could be done for us in that town and what resources it could offer. When I arrived at the gate I found a congestion and confusion comparable to the passage of the Beresina. No precaution had been taken to restore order; and while people fought at the gate, there were open passages near it which none knew of and none indicated. I succeeded in entering by fighting my way through the mob. When I reached the center of the town I was unable to learn where the Third Corps was to be located. At the governor's residence and the town hall all was confusion. Night came; I had no idea where my regiment was. Overcome with exhaustion, I entered the lodgings of the Prince of Neuchâtel, whose servants had all scattered; and after having dined on a jar of preserves without bread, I went to sleep on a plank and postponed my search until the next day.

7 By way of Byenitsa and Smorgon.

CHAPTER EIGHT

State of the army in Vilna

Withdrawal of the King of Naples

Attack of the Russians

Hastened departure

Charged with the rear guard

March to Kovno

AT DAWN I WENT THROUGH THE town again, seeking news of my regiment. The spectacle which Vilna offered then resembled nothing we had seen until that time. All the country through which we had just passed bore the imprint of that destruction of which we were both the authors and the victims. The towns were burned and their inhabitants in flight; the few of them who remained shared our misery, and a divine malediction seemed to have touched all around us with death. But at Vilna the houses still stood; their inhabitants went about their ordinary occupations. Everywhere we saw a rich and populous city, and through this city wandered our ragged, starving soldiers. Some paid gold for the meanest food; others sought a piece of bread from the charity of the inhabitants. The latter looked with horror upon the remains of that army, once so formidable, which had excited their admiration five months before. The Poles lamented the misfortunes which now dashed their hopes; the partisans of Russia were triumphant; the merchants saw only an opportunity to make us pay more dearly for what we needed. The shops,

State of the army in Vilna

inns, and cafés, unable to accommodate the quantity of purchasers, were closed from the first day. The inhabitants, who feared our avidity would soon lead to a famine, took to hiding their provisions. The army had stores of all sorts at Vilna; some distributions were made to the Guard, but the rest of the army was in too great a disorder to take part. As for military dispositions, none were taken. Indeed, what could be done? To defend Vilna would be to attempt the impossible; to withdraw was to act against the intentions of the Emperor. In this situation the King of Naples made no preparations either for defense or for the evacuation of the town, whose approaches were still being guarded by General Loison.

By dint of much searching I found Marshal Ney's quarters, and I learned from him that the Second and Third Corps had been billeted in a convent in the Smolensk suburb; I went there immediately, or rather as rapidly as the mounting congestion in the streets would permit. The enemy, but feebly checked by General Loison, drew close to the town. We could hear the sound of cannon, and the Smolensk gate was crowded with stragglers, some already wounded by enemy lances, who struggled desperately to clear a passage for themselves. It took all my strength to push my way into the suburb. The Third Corps had in fact occupied the day before the convent that had been pointed out to me; but all the officers as well as the generals had dispersed; there remained only a sergeant and ten men from my regiment, and they did not know where any of the officers were quartered. Incredible as it is to believe, at this moment two aides-de-camp of General Hogendorp, Governor of Vilna, brought orders to the Second and Third Corps to take arms and move into the line to support General Loison; they found only a few unarmed men, half-frozen and sick, without officers or generals. Far from obeying such a bizarre order, I told the sergeant to enter the town if the enemy entered the suburb. I returned there immediately myself, risking the terrible press a third time. The sound of cannon which drew nearer created new alarm. The long roll was beaten; Marshal Lefebvre and several generals rode through the streets shouting "to arms!" A few squads headed toward the Smolensk gate; but the greater number of soldiers, lying in the streets or in the houses where they were given entry, declared that they could fight no more, and that they would stay where they were. The townspeople, fearful of pillage, hastened to shut up their houses and bar their doors. The Old Guard, which alone was still in good order, formed in the square, and I joined it. At nightfall calm returned, the cannon ceased to fire, and the Loison Division remained in position on the heights around the town. The King of Naples did not wish to run the risk of being overwhelmed a second time; that same evening he moved to the Kovno suburb, which he left before dawn. I returned to Marshal Ney's headquarters, where I received the order to depart. The Third Corps left the next day at six o'clock in the morning under the command of General Marchand; Marshal Ney was destined to save what remained of the army to the very last. He took over once again the command of the rear guard, composed of the Bavarians (Sixth Corps) and the Loison Division.

Shortly afterwards an officer of my regiment sought me out and led me to the major's lodgings, and I rejoined my regiment from which I had been separated in such an unusual manner for two days. How true it is that in war one always regrets having left his post, even with the authorization of one's superiors, and with the best of intentions! The officers of the Fourth, like the rest of the army, had spent the day peacefully in nearby houses, little concerned by the alarm or the enemy's approach. A captain had just arrived from Nancy (the regiment's depot) with

Hastened departure

clothing and footwear. A distribution was made to the officers and men present, but the remainder was to be abandoned for lack of transport. I decided to sell them to a merchant and ordered the officer who had brought them to stay behind until the departure of the rear guard and conclude the sale. This officer, who was very anxious about the situation in Vilna, had no desire to prolong his stay; and after several objections which I found very offensive, he did not hesitate to disobey me, and indeed he left ahead of us. This officer had ruined himself forever in my eyes; in justice to his memory I should add that later he perished on the field of battle.

The King of Naples left at four in the morning with the Old Guard and the remains of the various army corps followed in succession. They say that Marshal Mortier learned of the departure quite by chance and marched off with the Young Guard without having received any orders. As for ourselves, we left at six o'clock with General Marchand. Several hours later Marshal Ney evacuated the town, which was immediately occupied by the Russian advance guard. We left there stores of food, arms, and clothing. Several generals, many officers, and more than 20,000 men, nearly all of them ill, fell into the hands of the enemy; these unfortunates had spent all their strength in reaching Vilna, believing they would find some repose there. When the rear guard left, the inhabitants massacred and robbed all those they came upon; the rest died of neglect in hospitals or were led into the interior of Russia. Thus we lost this city which had been so gloriously conquered at the beginning of the campaign.

There were still twenty-six leagues to go in order to cross the Niemen at Kovno, and we had not a moment to lose, for the day spent in Vilna had given the Russians a great advantage. That day had been passed in knocking on the doors of houses to beg for bread, and since the little food that we had found was now consumed, we had nothing to take with us even had transport been available. Thus the same calamities I have already described continued to befall us, and our wasted strength would not permit us to withstand them much longer.

A league from Vilna is a large mountain whose steep incline was covered with ice; that mountain was as fatal for our baggage as the passage of the Beresina had been. The horses made useless efforts to ascend it, and we could save neither vehicles nor cannon. Along the side of the road we saw all the artillery of the Guard, the rest of the Emperor's baggage, and the treasury of the army. As the soldiers passed, they broke into the wagons and loaded themselves down with rich clothing, furs, and gold and silver coin. It was a strange spectacle to see men covered with gold and yet dying of hunger, and to see scattered in the snow of Russia all the luxurious commodities of Paris. The pillage continued until the Cossacks fell on the looters and seized all those riches.

My companions had been obliged to disperse and pick their way through the abandoned wagons and teams; when I reached the summit there was not a single one with me, but several joined me during the march. One of my battalion chiefs, who was ill and on a sled, disappeared forever. The first day we made nine leagues, the second we made seven, to Zhizhmory. I had lost General Marchand and was leading the regiment by myself. The officers asked me to stop one league farther back; but there were ten leagues from Zhizhmory to Kovno, and the approaching cannon of the rear guard told me that we had to reach Kovno on the following day. Thus I insisted that we go as far as Zhizhmory, where some huts filled with wounded offered shelter.

The next day, the 12th, I set out again at five in the morning. The darkness of the night and the ice on the road made this march very difficult. At daybreak an officer came to tell me that Marshal Ney and the rear guard had passed through Zhizhmory during the night and were ahead of us, and that nothing separated us from the enemy. That moment was for me the most terrible of the entire campaign. I looked about me: twenty enfeebled officers, the same number of soldiers, half of them without arms—that was my entire regiment, all there were to defend our life and freedom. We were marching to the Niemen, and now in this final moment we would lose the goal of two months of suffering, of so much devotion and so much great sacrifice. The thought of this almost took away all my courage. I hastened the march, giving no thought to my own fatigue or that of my companions, heedless of the slippery ground on which we fell at each step. I had passed along this road several times in the month of June, after the crossing of the Niemen. Then in the most delightful season of the year, it had been filled with great numbers of troops, as admirable for their ardor and enthusiasm as for their magnificent appearance. And now along the same road there passed a crowd of ragged, fleeing men, without strength and without courage, tottering with fatigue, trying to run away from an enemy they could no longer fight. This terrible contrast struck me deeply; and though I was overcome with exhaustion, I felt keenly the depth of our misfortune.

We were halfway to Kovno when I learned positively that Marshal Ney and the rear guard were still behind us. This news, which calmed my anxiety, also enabled me to give my regiment a few moments of rest in the ruins of the village of Rykonti; afterwards we strove again to reach Kovno, which seemed to retreat before us. Two officers who were being pulled along in a sled offered to take me with them, but I refused in order to encourage my companions by my example. I believe that it was some measure of my worth that I did not accept that offer; never had I been so exhausted, and more than once I almost fell by the wayside. Finally we caught sight of the Niemen again and entered Kovno. While the soldiers went to seek rum and biscuits I collapsed against a curbstone. There were no lodgings to be found. I had to force my way with my officers into a house occupied by the Fourth Corps, who did not want to accept us; we all slept on the floor.

Marshal Ney arrived after having left a part of the rear guard before the town. General Marchand rejoined us that evening with the other regiments: he gave us orders to depart the next morning at five o'clock. We were to cross the Niemen and leave forever this land of misfortunes. But at the moment of departure Marshal Ney decided that we should remain with him in the rear guard. This final test of courage and devotion required of us was to be among the most difficult. For some time those who remained of the Third Corps had come to think they had fulfilled their task: they had reached the Niemen, and although they were no longer in condition to fight, they were now being told to remain in Kovno to try to defend it, or rather to perish honorably in its ruins. I must say, however, to the credit of the officers and men, that each obeyed without a murmur, and that none left his post in so critical a situation. As for me, having seen the steadfast heroism of Marshal Ney, I congratulated myself on being given the honor to second his final efforts; we returned to our quarters, awaiting further orders and ready for any eventuality.

KOVNO, LIKE VILNA, WAS FILLED with storehouses, and as might be expected, the distributions were not well made here. But the soldiers were no longer willing to die of hunger in the midst of plenty. The storehouses that had been respected at Vilna were pilfered at Kovno, and this new disorder brought new evils in turn; many men who had drunk too much rum were overcome by the cold and died. This drink was all the more dangerous for them since they did not know its effects, and being accustomed to the miserable *eau-de-vie* of the country, they thought they could drink rum in equally large quantities. They stove in the barrels and the rum flowed in the storehouses and even in the streets; other soldiers carried off biscuits or divided up sacks of flour. The doors to the clothing depots were opened and the clothing thrown about. Each soldier took what he could find and dressed in the middle of the street; but most of them, passing through Kovno without stopping, gave thought only to flight. Accustomed to follow mechanically those who marched before them, they risked death on the congested bridges without thinking that they could easily walk across the frozen Niemen.

CHAPTER NINE

Situation at Kovno

Defense of the town

Passage of the Niemen

Last attack of the Russians

Ney's presence of mind

March to Koenigsberg

Cantonments on the Vistula

Arrival at Marienburg

Part Two, Chapter Nine

Meanwhile Marshal Ney sought to defend Kovno in order to give these wretches the time to escape the enemy's pursuit, and also to protect the retreat of the King of Naples, who had taken the Koenigsberg road by way of Gumbinnen the day before. Hastily constructed earthworks before the Vilna gate seemed to him a sufficient defense to hold the enemy the entire day. In the morning the rear guard entered the city; two pieces of cannon supported by a few squads of Bavarian infantry were placed on the rampart, and this small body of troops prepared to withstand the attack which was already being prepared. When Marshal Ney had made his dispositions he went to repose in his quarters; he had scarcely gone when the fighting began. The first Russian cannon shots dismantled one of our pieces; the infantry took flight and the artillerymen were about to follow them. The Cossacks were about to enter the town unchallenged when the Marshal appeared on the rampart. His absence was almost our undoing; his presence sufficed to save us. He took up a musket, the troops returned to their posts, and the battle recommenced and kept up until evening, when the retreat began. Thus this last success was due to the personal bravery of the Marshal, who fought like a common soldier for the position whose preservation he considered so important.

I only learned later of the danger we had risked, and I would have regretted not being with the Marshal, had my first duty not been with my regiment; we spent that day, as well as the 18th, in the house of a merchant where we found some food and much brandy. This sort of abundance also had its dangers, for after so much privation the least excess could be fatal. In spite of Colonel Pelleport's warning and my own, several men got drunk and could not follow us. The officers found their trunks at Kovno; since there was no way of transporting them, each took what he could use and abandoned the rest, all too happy at saving his life to think of regrets.

Toward evening the order to depart arrived: the Third Corps was to open the march, followed by the Bavarians and what was left of the Loison Division. We passed through Kovno amid the dead and dying. By the light of the campfires still burning in the streets we could see soldiers who watched us pass with indifference; and when we told them that they would fall into the hands of the enemy, they lowered their heads and bent over the fires without replying. The inhabitants who lined the street looked at us insolently. One of them had already armed himself with a musket which I took away from him. Several soldiers who had dragged themselves to the Niemen fell dead on the bridge, just at the moment they were reaching the end of their misery. We crossed the stream and looking back toward the frightful country we were leaving, we congratulated ourselves on having quitted it and on the honor of having been the last to do so.

On the other side of the Niemen the Gumbinnen road traverses a high mountain. Scarcely had we reached the foot of it when some soldiers who were preceding us came running back telling us that they had encountered Cossacks. At that very moment a cannon ball fell in our ranks, and we knew for certain that the Cossacks had crossed the frozen Niemen, seized the height with their artillery, and thus blocked our retreat. This last attack, the most unexpected of all, was the one which most overwhelmed the soldiers. During the retreat the idea became widely held that the Russians would not cross the Niemen. As soon as they were on the other side of the bridge, all thought themselves perfectly safe, as if the Niemen were like that river of the ancients which separated the earth from the underworld. One can therefore understand what terror seized them upon finding themselves pursued on the other side and enemy artillery on the road before them. Generals Marchand and Ledru managed to form a sort of battalion by incorporating into the Third Corps all the isolated soldiers who could be found. They tried in vain to force a passage; the soldiers' muskets would not reach the enemy and they themselves did not dare advance. We had to abandon any such attempt and remain under the artillery fire without daring to retire, for to do so was to expose ourselves to a charge, and that would certainly be the end of us. This situation produced complete despair in two officers who had been an example to my regiment during the entire retreat; their last strength was gone, leaving their courage shaken. They came and told me that since we could neither fight nor move we would fall into the hands of the Cossacks who would massacre us, and therefore they were going to return to Kovno to surrender. I tried in vain to restrain them: I reminded them of their sense of honor, of the courage that they had so often displayed, and of their attachment for the regiment they were abandoning; and, if their death were inevitable, I urged them at least to die with us. Their only response was to embrace me with tears in their eyes and return to Kovno. Two other officers suffered the same fate: one got drunk with rum and could not follow us; the other, of whom I was particularly fond, disappeared shortly afterward. I was much grieved at this, and I expected death to reunite me with my unfortunate comrades; indeed I might have welcomed this, had there not been so many bonds still attaching me to life.

Marshal Ney appeared at this juncture, showing not the slightest concern over such a desperate situation. His prompt determination saved us again and for the last time. He decided to descend the Niemen and take the road to Tilsit, hoping to reach Koenigsberg by back roads. He did not conceal the danger of leaving the Gumbinnen road, thus leaving the rest of the army without a rear guard—a danger all the more grave since there was no way to alert the King of Naples. But there was no other way, and necessity determined our duty. The darkness of the night favored this movement. Two leagues from Kovno we left the banks of the Niemen to take a road through woods to our left, a road that was to take us to Koenigsberg. We lost many soldiers who had no warning and were marching singly and who followed the Niemen to Tilsit. During that night and the next day we scarcely stopped to rest. A white horse which we took turns riding bareback was a tremendous help to us. On the evening of the 14th we took shelter in a good-sized village. There I lost two more officers: one died during the night in the chamber where I slept and the other disappeared the next day. These were the last of our misfortunes, for from that day on, our situation changed radically. The rapidity of our march had put us far in advance; moreover, the Cossacks were busy pursuing the other corps on the main road. Since the mountain at Kovno we had seen them no more. The country through which we passed had not been ravaged, and we found food and vehicles. Marshal Ney went directly to Koenigsberg[1] where we rejoined him on the 20th, still led by General Marchand.

One must bear in mind how much we suffered in order to understand how happy we were in those first days of abundance; looking at us, one would be more apt to pity us than to envy us. The Third Corps was composed of about one hundred soldiers on foot, led by a few officers, and a similar number of incapacitated men of all ranks, borne on sleds. The cold was excessive, and we used any means to protect ourselves from it. Thus the inhabitants, and particularly the merchants, sold us the most

---

1 By way of Neustadt, Pillkahlen, and Saliau.

ordinary clothing for their weight in gold; for they believed us loaded with the treasures of Moscow. As we traversed the old Mark of Prussia, it was not difficult to see how the inhabitants felt toward us. There was a malignant curiosity in their questions, and ironic lamentations over our sufferings, or false news about the Cossacks, whom we never saw, but who were always about to appear. If a soldier left the road he was disarmed by the peasants and driven off with threats and ill treatment. A Protestant minister even went so far as to tell me that our misfortunes were God's just punishment for having plundered and ravaged our Prussian ally. I must say that we were little offended by this hostile reception: the joy of finding food and sleeping in well-heated chambers made up for all.

The King of Naples, thinking Marshal Ney in his rear, had gone from Kovno to Koenigsberg by the Gumbinnen road. An officer whom he sent on a mission to the Marshal fell into the hands of the Cossacks; by some miracle he got away again and brought back word that the rear guard was destroyed, and nothing held back the enemy. The King of Naples hastened his march and arrived in Koenigsberg before us. This town was already filled with generals, officers, civilians, and stray soldiers who arrived pell-mell to profit from the resources the city offered. The inns and taverns could not serve all the customers; officers were seen to spend the entire night at the table, and then to succumb to intemperance after they had resisted hunger. The shops were besieged with buyers. Gems and other precious objects brought from Moscow were now sold in great haste, and their value was so great that soon all the gold in the town had been spent on them, even though the inhabitants (whose insolence toward us was extreme) used every means to profit from our situation. The first care of the King of Naples when he arrived in

Koenigsberg was to try to restore order to an army given over to such confusion. Circumstances seemed favorable, for Marshal MacDonald with the Tenth Corps had evacuated Courland and taken a position on the Niemen at Tilsit, covering the rest of the army; he still had 30,000 men, counting the Prussians. The King of Naples directed the remains of the army corps to the following cantonments: the First Corps at Thorn, the Second and Third at Marienburg, the Fourth at Marienwerder, the Fifth at Warsaw, the Sixth at Plock, the Seventh at Wengrov, the Ninth at Danzig, and the Austrians at Ostroleka, the cavalry at Elbing, the Guard and headquarters at Koenigsberg. Once these cantonments were designated, a very severe directive ordered all the generals and officers who were in Koenigsberg without authorization to leave within twenty-four hours. Some of these, by their dejected air and ill-considered remarks, had helped to ruin us in the eyes of the inhabitants. A second order stated that anyone who crossed the Vistula would be regarded as a deserter to the enemy.

I have said that the Third Corps arrived at Koenigsberg on the 20th. We continued our march the next day. Marshal Ney remained at headquarters and General Marchand, who was destined for another command, did not accompany us; since the few generals and colonels who survived had gone on ahead, I led the Third Corps myself in the five days' march to Marienburg.[2] Barely thirty men of my regiment and a hundred and twenty of the Third Corps reached this destination together. At Marienburg we rejoined generals Ledru, Joubert, and d'Hénin, as well as the officers and men who had made their way there separately. Many of them still had that frightened air that bespoke the dangers they had run, although they had aban-

---

[2] By way of Heiligenbeil and Elbing.

Part Two, Chapter Nine

doned us long before in order to leave those dangers all the sooner. We received cantonments in the villages of Nogat Island. The regiments went there on the 26th, and we prepared to use this repose to reassemble the human debris of the great tragedy and to repair as soon as possible the damage that had been done.

CHAPTER TEN

Sojourn on the Vistula
Defection of the Prussians
Retreat to the Oder
Disbanding the army
Results of the campaign
Conclusion

NOGAT ISLAND IS A KIND OF DELTA formed by the two arms of the Vistula and the sea; that country is full of good villages, and we were well placed there for reorganizing our regiments. The first days of rest were delightful indeed after two and a half months of privation and fatigue, and we took all the advantage we could of those precious moments. We immediately went to work on the replacement of shoes and uniforms. Each day came the arrival of some straggling soldier whom we thought lost forever; my surgeon-major, whom I had been lucky enough to retain, picked out those who were no longer fit for service and they were sent to the rear. As for the others, a few days of rest restored their strength. At the same time I resumed the correspondence so long interrupted with the major at Nancy. The cold was as violent as ever, but we no longer feared it; snugly quartered in the houses of the peasants and sharing their coarse food, we seemed to be enjoying all the pleasures of life. The long evenings we spent in telling anecdotes of the campaign and in writing to our families, who were still five hundred leagues away, and much alarmed by the Twenty-ninth Bulletin.

Part Two, Chapter Ten

During this cantonment I went to Danzig, only some twelve leagues away: there we found in abundance all that we had not had the time to procure in Koenigsberg. General Rapp was preparing its defense in case the army should continue its retreat. In a short time the town was provisioned and the ramparts armed.

Fifteen days had been spent in the cantonments and the regiments had begun to form again; the Fourth had gathered two hundred men when an unexpected event changed our position. General Yorck with his Prussian corps was serving as the rear guard for Marshal MacDonald before Tilsit. On the 30th of December he signed an agreement with the Russians and became a neutral. Marshal MacDonald lost more than half the Tenth Corps by this defection and was obliged to retire toward Koenigsberg with the Russians following him. It was no longer possible to hold the line of the Vistula for we were not in a position to defend it; already several bands of Cossacks had created alarm in Marienburg and Marienwerder. Some even crossed the Vistula on the ice and sought to disturb our cantonments. The King of Naples left Koenigsberg on January 9 and went to Elbing. The retreat along the line of the Oder and the Warta was decided. The Tenth Corps was made part of the garrison of Danzig, which was thereby increased to 30,000 men, and the other corps began their retreat. The First Corps moved toward Stelton, the Second and Third toward Küstrin, and the Fourth and Sixth toward Posen. On the night of the 10th of January the Third Corps assembled at Dirschau and crossed the western arm of the Vistula. Of the two hundred men who composed my regiment barely forty were armed, and the officer who had gone to seek muskets at Danzig only got to our cantonment the next day. Fortunately he learned of our movement and rejoined us on the road on the 11th, having adroitly dodged the Cossacks.

Retreat to the Oder

The first day of march the assembled Third Corps numbered nearly 1,000 men armed and fairly well clothed. Marshal Ney reappeared at our head and expressed himself as satisfied over the measures we had taken. Soon afterwards he left us to return to France. The Third Corps arrived at Küstrin on January 20, [1] skirting the frontiers of the Grand Duchy of Warsaw. General Ledru directed the march as commander-in-chief and General d'Hénin commanded the Second Division; there were no other generals left. The attitude of the inhabitants was uniformly unfavorable to us, but they expressed themselves less openly since we were now more to be feared. Some sought to pay court to us by loudly denouncing General Yorck's defection; others sought to alarm us with false reports about the Russian pursuit. These schemes were of little avail: we knew that the enemy infantry could not reach us, and as for the Cossacks, we ceased to fear them once we were armed again. On one occasion, however, a general was told that Cossacks were near him in force, and from prudence he abandoned the village he was occupying with a regiment. It is said that this false report was instigated by the master of a chateau where the general stayed, and who desired to get rid of his guest. I remember also that as we approached Küstrin my regiment was lodged in a village with a regiment of Spaniards and one of Illyrians; a singular chance thus united in the same place men from such diverse nations, and for a cause so foreign to the interests of their countries.

The retreat of the other corps was carried out as tranquilly as ours. When we arrived at Posen the Viceroy took command of the entire army, a post which had become vacant with the departure of the King of Naples. The right wing, composed of the Austrians and the Seventh Corps, still defended the Vistula near Warsaw; but already Prince

[1] By way of Stargard, Driessen, and Landsberg.

Part Two, Chapter Ten

Schwartzenberg was preparing to return to Galicia, maintaining neutrality, while the King of Prussia only awaited the arrival of the Russians at Berlin in order to join them. Soon the Viceroy would be forced to retire behind the Oder, or even the Elbe, until the arrival of reinforcements coming from France and Italy.

Meanwhile the Emperor was busy in Paris with the reorganization of the regiments, but the orders he issued prove that he was not aware of the extent to which the regiments had been destroyed. At first he wanted to send the cadres of the fourth battalion back to France and leave the three others with the army; then he decided to send back the third and fourth while keeping the first two. The officers pointed out that none of this could be executed, and on their representations it was decided to recall all the cadres to the depots, leaving only the able-bodied men with the army. Each regiment formed companies of a hundred men in condition to fight, commanded by three officers; these companies were to be re-formed into provisional battalions to defend the fortresses along the Oder such as Küstrin, Stettin, and Spandau. The Third Corps provided in this fashion a battalion of six hundred men destined to form the garrison of Spandau. It was very difficult for me to leave the hundred men of my regiment who were to take part. I promised them on leaving that if peace did not bring them back to France soon, we would return to deliver them—a prediction which events did not bear out. The next day what remained of the regiments set out for France. A hundred men of the Fourth, including officers, non-commissioned officers, and invalid soldiers, left Küstrin for the regiment's depot at Nancy.

This period, which was one of reorganization of the regiments, brings to a close all that is relative to the campaign of 1812. At that time I could no longer think of anything but rejoining my family; and leaving to the major the task of leading the regiment, I took the post carriage to Mainz, by way of Berlin and Magdeburg. Marshal Kellermann, who commanded at Mainz, gave me permission to go to Nancy and visit the depot of my regiment.

I will not attempt to describe my joy at finding myself once again in France and hearing French being spoken around me; to understand my feelings one would have had to have travelled equally far.

At Nancy I received a touching welcome. The officers of the depot battalion expressed their gratitude for the care I had taken of the regiment during the terrible retreat; they all told me that they regretted being separated from their comrades and unable to share their glory and honorable reverses. I found the battalion well trained and imposing in appearance; the administration, which was directed by an excellent quartermaster,[2] left nothing to be desired. I had nothing but praise for the major,[3] a very distinguished officer whose advancement I was later able to second. Three days had been passed in such occupations when I received the authorization to go to Paris. One can well imagine that I lost no time in doing so. But to make the misfortune that attended my travels complete, my carriage broke down several leagues from Paris. Arriving in the middle of the night, riding on a hay wagon and wrapped in a wolf skin, I at last stood before the house I had left nine months before in the midst of such immense preparations and of such hopes for success and glory.

All of us who had the possibility to do so spent some time with our families, but we found no happiness there. Horrible memories troubled our minds; the spectres of the victims of that campaign did not cease to pursue us, and

2   M. Goudonville.
3   M. Boni.

Part Two, Chapter Ten

our hearts were filled with a deep sadness that all the cares of loved ones could not dispel.

Thus ended this gigantic enterprise which had begun under such propitious signs. Its results were the total destruction of an army of 500,000 men with all its services and its immense materiel. Barely 70,000 men recrossed the Vistula; the number of prisoners was only 100,000 hence 300,000 perished.[4] These frightful figures are in agreement with the reports of the Russian authorities charged with cremating the bodies of our men, of which they counted nearly 300,000. The entire artillery, composed of 1,200 pieces and their caissons, was taken or abandoned, as well as 3,000 wagons, the baggage of the officers and stores of all kinds. History offers no other example of such a disaster, and this journal can give but a feeble idea of its extent; but at least I have written enough to preserve the memory of the events which I witnessed, some of which are little known. Of those who read what I have written I ask only that they share the emotions which I feel as I conclude this account: I ask them to join me in admiration for so much courage and sorrow for so much misfortune.

The end.

Note: The reader will permit me here to copy an extract of a letter from Marshal Ney to the Duke of Feltre, the original of which I have preserved. The reader will understand the value I attach to its testimony:

---

4 I have said that 500,000 men took part in the campaign in its entirety or in part. If one subtracts 80,000 men for the three corps which formed the two wings (the Seventh and the Austrians on the right wing and the Tenth on the left), the total for the Grand Army comes to 420,000. Of these the number which recrossed the Vistula was at the very most 10,000, almost all sick and disabled. Thus we lost 410,000. As for the three detached corps, which suffered less, their losses could not have been less than 20,000 men. Thus the total casualties were 430,000.

Conclusion

Berlin, January 23rd, 1813
Monsieur le duc, I profit from this moment in which the campaign, if not terminated, is at least suspended, to tell you all the satisfaction I have felt with M. de Fezensac's service. This young man has found himself in very serious circumstances and has always risen above them. I present him to you as a true French knight, and you may henceforth regard him as an old colonel.

Signed: M^{al} Duc d'Elchingen

APPENDICES

APPENDIX A

*Table containing the Enumeration
and Disposition of the Forces led
into the Russian Empire by Napoleon*

*Napoleon, Emperor of the French
Marshal Berthier, Chief of Staff*

	INFANTRY	CAVALRY
FIRST CORPS *Marshal Prince of Eckmühl* FRENCH DIVISIONS: Morand, Friand, Gudin, Desaix and Compans—	65,000	
LIGHT BRIGADES: Bordesoulle and Pajol—		2,400
SECOND CORPS *Marshal Duke of Reggio* FRENCH DIVISIONS: Legrand, Verdier, and Merle—	32,000	
LIGHT BRIGADES: Castex and Corbineau—		2,400
THIRD CORPS *Marshal Duke of Elchingen* FRENCH DIVISIONS: Ledru and Razout; WÜRTTEMBERGER DIVISION: Marchand—	35,000	
LIGHT BRIGADES: Mouriez and Beurmann—		2,400
FOURTH CORPS *Viceroy of Italy* FRENCH DIVISIONS: Delzons and Broussier; ITALIAN ROYAL GUARD; ITALIAN DIVISION: Pino—	38,000	
CAVALRY OF THE ITALIAN GUARD; ITALIAN LIGHT BRIGADE: Villata—		2,400

Appendix A

	INFANTRY	CAVALRY
FIFTH CORPS *Prince Poniatowski*		
POLISH DIVISIONS: Dombrowski, Zayonschek, and Ficher—	36,000	
LIGHT CAVALRY—		2,400
SIXTH CORPS *General, then Marshal Gouvion-Saint-Cyr*		
BAVARIAN DIVISIONS: Deroy and De Wrede—	25,000	
BAVARIAN LIGHT BRIGADES: Seidewitz and Preisseing—		2,400
SEVENTH CORPS *General Count Reynier*		
SAXON DIVISIONS: Lecocq and Zeschau—	24,000	
LIGHT CAVALRY: Funck and Gablentz—		2,400
EIGHTH CORPS *General Duke of Abrantès*		
WESTPHALIAN DIVISIONS: Ochs and de Dareau—	18,000	
LIGHT CAVALRY—		1,200
NINTH CORPS *Marshal Duke of Bellune*		
DIVISIONS: Partonneaux, Daendels, and Girard—	30,000	2,500
TENTH CORPS *Marshal Duke of Tarente*		
FRENCH DIVISION: Grandjean; PRUSSIAN CORPS: Yorck, composed of Kleist and Grawert Divisions, 20 battalions of infantry—	26,000	
PRUSSIAN LIGHT CAVALRY: Massenbach—		3,000
IMPERIAL GUARD		
OLD GUARD, commanded by the *Marshal Duke of Danzig*; YOUNG GUARD, commanded by the *Marshal Duke of Trévise*—	32,000	
CAVALARY OF THE GUARD, *commanded by the Marshal Duke of Istria*—		3,800

Appendix A

CAVALRY RESERVE

First Corps
General Nansouty
Bruyères, Saint-Germain, and Valence Divisions—   7,200

Second Corps
Watier, Sebastiani, and Defrance Divisions—   7,200

Third Corps
General Grouchy

Fourth Corps
General Latour-Maubourg

These two corps underwent several changes in their organization during the campaign, so they are listed *en bloc*; they were composed of these divisions:

Kellermann, Lahoussaye, Chastel, Rosnitzky (Polish), and Thielmann (Saxon); in all—   12,000
The Doumerc Division (5th Cuirassiers) was detached with the Second Corps—   2,300

Austrian Corps
(which may be counted as the eleventh corps)
General, later Marshal Prince Schwartzemberg
AUSTRIAN DIVISIONS: Sicgenthal, Trantenburg and Bianchi—   24,000
CAVALRY DIVISION: Frimont—   6,000

385,000   62,000

447,000

APPENDIX B

I WILL MAKE NO DETAILED DESCRIPTION OF MOSCOW HERE, FOR I knew only its destruction; I will only say a few words on its construction and the manners of its inhabitants. The Prince de Ligne depicted Moscow in a manner as accurate as it was piquant when he said that it was fifty villages grouped around three hundred chateaux.

Moscow is divided into four zones; in the center is the Kremlin, antique citadel which contains a superb palace and several churches, and tombs of the emperors, not far from the place where they were crowned. All of the structures are bizarre, and it would be difficult to say to what order of architecture they belong. From the top of the citadel travelers used to enjoy contemplating this immense city, which today no longer offers anything to our eyes but a vast expanse or ruins.

Around the Kremlin is the Chinese town, the quarter inhabited by the merchants. There was located the bazaar, which was the first victim of the flames. This quarter is the immense rendezvous of merchants from all the countries of Europe and Asia.

The white town surrounds the Chinese town. It is the quarter of the nobility and the one in which the most magnificent town houses are found. Finally, the earthen town is the last part; it is really a vast circular suburb which surrounds Moscow: there are enclosures, large gardens, even cultivated fields, and the cottages of peasants next to magnificent palaces. The houses are in general built of wood, some on runners so that they may be moved; the churches and many mansions are of brick; most of the roofs are of painted sheet metal.

As I have indicated earlier, the inhabitants of Moscow, like those of the rest of Russia, are divided into three classes: the nobles, the merchants, and the peasants. The nobles exercise over their peasants an almost sovereign authority; they can inflict cor-

Appendix B

poral punishment on them and prohibit them from marrying. They fix the tax they should pay and designate those who must march when the emperor orders a levy of men. If the Russian lords are considered in their private life, they are found to be well endowed with taste, elegance, and magnificence; they are fond of the arts, curious about anything that is new and rare; among them one finds a luxury unknown today in the rest of Europe. There is, for example, a certain great lord who maintains two or three hundred servants. They have horn music, which unfortunately exists scarcely anywhere.[1] Their hospitality can be compared to no other; a foreigner becomes their friend in an instant. But it would be a mistake to trust too much in this kindly reception, for there is in their character such a fund of bizarreness and frivolity that suddenly one may very innocently fall into disgrace in their eyes, and then one can expect to be mistreated by them as he was previously overwhelmed with kindnesses.

The merchants of Russia form a special class: they are free but they may own no slaves; those of Moscow enjoy great privileges. The commerce of the town is considerable. The merchants can be recognized by their long belted robes; nearly all of them wear beards.

The Russian peasants are happy: their lords treat them well customarily, and always come to their aid in case of fire or bad harvests; thus they do not aspire to a liberty that they do not understand, and that they would not know what to do with. They have few ideas, and consequently few needs. Their clothing is composed of a robe of coarse cloth and sandals of birch bark; they bathe often. Their huts are as simple as those of the Polish peasants, but not so dirty; the top of the stove serves as a bed. The whole family sleeps there pell-mell. Their food is crude and healthful; it is composed of rye bread, vegetables, and sour drinks. They are religious and indeed superstitious.

---

[1] The reference is undoubtedly to that curious instrument, the Russian horn. Since it was capable of producing only one tone, there was a horn for each tone in the scale—and a horn player. These brass ensembles, generally of thirty-seven members, were popular in the second half of the eighteenth century. The time that had to be consumed in training and practice can well be imagined. Such an orchestra could only be feasible in a country with a tradition of servility and manpower to waste. [Ed.]

APPENDIX C

*Exact Account of the Losses
of the Fourth Regiment*

SOLDIERS

2150 men crossed the Rhine; a detachment of 400 men joined us at Moscow; another of equal size at Smolensk; finally, one of 50 men at Vilna; total, 3000 men who made the campaign. Of these 3000 men, only 200 returned with me to the Vistula, and about a hundred came back from imprisonment; thus there was a loss of 2700 men out of 3000, that is, nine-tenths.

OFFICERS

109 officers of all grades made the campaign in whole or in part.
40 were killed or died in the retreat or in the enemy's prisons.
20 remained prisoners, most of them wounded.
35 were wounded, several twice.
14 were not wounded.
Thus 49 officers came back, 35 of them wounded in the course of the campaign.

APPENDIX D

Itinerary of the Third Corps during the Retreat

October	19	Departure from Moscow. Bivouac on the Chirkovo road
	20	Chirkovo
	23	Departure at midnight
	24	Bivouac on the Borovsk road
	25	Continuation of the march
	26	Borovsk
	27	Departure in the evening
	28	Morning at Vereya. Evening at Gorodok-Borisov
	29	Kolotsk Abbey. Road from Moscow to Smolensk
	30	Gzhatsk
November	1	Vyazma
	5	Semlevo
	6	Postvia-Dvor
	7	Dorogobuzh
	8	Battle at Dorogobuzh. Bivouac two leagues away
	10–11	Slopnevo (Battle the 11th)
	12	Bivouac on the road to Smolensk
	13	Bivouac near Smolensk
	14	Suburb of Smolensk
	15–16	Smolensk (Fight on the 15th)
	17	Korytnia
	18	Arrival before Krasnii (Battle). Passage of the Dnieper
	19–20	March on the right bank of the Dnieper
	21	Morning at Orsha. Evening at Koshanov
	22	Tolochin
	23	Bobr

Appendix D

24	Nacha
25	Nemants
26	Veselovo (Passage of the Beresina in the night)
27–28	Bivouac on the right bank of the river (Combat at the Beresina on the 28th)
29	Zembin
30	Kamen
December 1	Bivouac in the direction of Molodechno
2	Ilia (Departure at night)
3	Molodechno
4	Smorgon
5	Byenitsa
6	Ozmiana
7	Miednicki
8–9	Vilna
10	Bivouac on the Kovno road
11	Zhizhmory
12	Kovno
13	Departure in the evening. Night march
14	Village in the direction of Neustadt
15	Neustadt
16	Pillkahlen
17	Rohr
18	Saliau
19	Tapiau
20	Koenigsberg
21	Braunsberg
22	Heiligenbeil
23	Neuenkirchen
24	Near Elbing
25	Marienburg
26	Cantonment on the Island of Nogat

INDEX

Abrantès, Jean-Andoche Junot, Duke of, 25
Alexander I, 3, 5, 20, 28, 42
Astorg, Adrien d', 12
Astorg, Eugene d', 12
Augereau, Pierre-François-Charles, General, 67

Babinovichi, 15
Bagration, Peter, Prince, 6, 7, 8, 13, 14, 15, 16, 19, 32
Bassano, Hugues-Bernard Maret, Duke of, 9
Barclay de Tolly, Michael, General, 7, 8, 14, 15, 16, 19, 22, 24
Beausset, M. de. 30
Bellune, Claude-Victor Perrin, Duke of, 91, 95, 97, 100, 102
Bérenger, M. de, 48
Berthier, Louis-Alexandre. *See* Neuchâtel, Prince of
Beshenkovichi, 14
Beurmann, General, 53, 58
Bessières, Jean-Baptiste, Marshal, 53
Bobr, 91
Bobruysk, 14
Bogorodsk, 46, 47
Bonaparte, Jerome, King of Westphalia, 13
Bonaparte, Joseph, 38
Bonaparte, Napoleon. *See* Napoleon
Borisov, 88, 89, 91, 92, 95
Borodino, 29, 30, 31, 32, 33, 55
Borovsk, 50, 52, 53, 54
Briqueville, M. de, 80

Castellane, M. de, 12
Caulaincourt, General, 33
Chabot, Fernand de, 12
Charpentier, General, 69

Index

Chashniki, 91
Chichagov, P. V., Admiral, 67, 91, 93, 94, 95, 96, 98, 102
Chirkovo, 52
Chotainski, 102
Colbert, General, 15
Compans, General, 29
Courland, 6, 7, 17, 121

Danzig, 9, 121, 124
Davout, Louis-Nicholas. *See* Eckmühl, Prince of
Dirschau, 124
Dmitrov, 46
Dokshitsy, 102
Dombrowski, General, 92
Dorogobuzh, 22, 27, 28, 60, 61, 63, 65
Dorsenne, General, 21
Dresden, 4
Drissa, 7, 8, 13, 14, 19
Dubrovno, 22
Dumas, Count, 10

Eckmühl, Louis-Nicholas Davout, Prince of, 14, 15, 55, 75, 86, 89
Elbing, 121, 124
Elnya, 50, 67

Fabvier, Colonel, 30
Feltre, Henri-Jacques-Guillaume Clarke, Duke of, 4, 128, 129
Flahaut, M. de, 12
Fominskoye, 50, 52
Friant, General, 21

Galicia, 125
Girardin, General, 53
Girardin, M. de, 12
Glubokoye, 12, 13, 14
Gorodok-Borisov, 54
Grodno, 6
Grouchy, Emmanuel de, General, 15
Gudin, General, 25
Gumbinnen, 5, 6
Gzhatsk, 28, 29, 56

Hénin, Etienne, General d': imprisonment in England, 38; reprimanded by Ney, 66; refuses to abandon his position, 82; wounded, 84; mentioned, 37, 62, 65, 81, 83, 85, 86, 121, 125

Index

Hogendorp, General, 109

Ilia, 101

Joubert, General, 38, 61, 62, 65, 121
Junot, Jean-Andoche. See Abrantès, Duke of

Kaluga, 43, 50, 52, 53
Kamen, 100
Kellermann, François-Christophe, Marshal, 127
Koenigsberg, 9, 118, 119, 120, 121, 124
Kolotsk Abbey, 55
Kopys, 92
Korytnia, 22, 75
Koshanov, 15
Kovno, 6, 7, 112, 113, 114, 115, 117, 118
Krasnii: battle of, 77–78; mentioned, 22, 75, 87, 94, 96, 139
Kremlin, 41
Kubinskoye, 37
Küstrin, 124, 125, 126
Kuskova, 44
Kutusov, Michael, General: succeeds General Barclay, 28; position at Borodino, 29; address to his troops, 31; retreats from Borodino, 32; forced to abandon Moscow, 40; blocks Napoleon's path, 43; at Maloyaroslavets, 53; mentioned, 92, 93, 102

Lalande, M., 84
Lanusse, M., 90
Lecouteulx, M., 12
Ledru des Essarts, General, 38, 86, 100, 103, 118, 121, 125
Lefebvre, François-Joseph, Duke of Danzig, 110
Lenchantin, General, 78
Lithuania, 8, 9, 10, 18, 26
Liubovichi, 81
Lobau, Count, 53, 101, 103
Loison, General, 109
Lyadi, 88

MacDonald, Alexandre, Marshal, 121, 124
Mainz, 127
Maloyaroslavets, 50, 53
Marchand, General, 37, 47, 110, 111, 112, 114, 118, 119, 121
Maret, Hugues-Bernard. *See* Bassano, Duke of
Marienburg, 121, 124
Marienwerder, 13, 121, 124

Index

Massy, Colonel, 33
Medyn, 50, 53
Miloradovich, General, 56, 57, 75, 77
Minsk, 13, 67, 69, 91, 99
Moghilev, 14, 15, 16, 17, 22, 50
Molodechno, 101, 102, 103
Montbrun, General, 33
Montesquiou, Anatole de, 12
Monthion, General, 10
Mortemart, M. de, 12
Mortier, Adolphe, Marshal, 51, 111
Moscow: burning of, 40–43; conditions in, 43–45; mentioned, 22, 28, 29, 30, 40, 41, 52, 89
Mozhaisk, 29, 37, 54
Murat, Joachim, King of Naples: opposes further advance, 26; leads advance guard to Moscow, 27; calls for peace or withdrawal, 46; given command of the army, 103; evacuates Vilna, 110–111; mentioned, 8, 15, 22, 23, 40, 43, 90, 109, 116, 119, 120, 121, 125

Nacha, 91
Nancy, 110, 123, 126, 127
Naples, King of. *See* Murat, Joachim
Napoleon: prepares invasion, 3–4; plans for Lithuania, 9, 18; concern for military administration, 21; desires a battle, 26; dispositions at Borodino, 29–30; proclamation to his troops, 31; visits battlefield of Borodino, 33; attempts to establish order in Moscow, 46; orders destruction of the city, 50–51; declines battle, 53; plans for crossing the Beresina, 93; leaves the army, 103; plans for rebuilding his army, 126; mentioned, 5, 8, 12, 15, 16, 28, 60, 70, 75, 86, 88, 90, 101
Narbonne, M. de, 5, 6, 19
Nemants, 91
Nememzin, 102
Neuchâtel, Louis-Alexandre Berthier, Prince of, 4, 10, 11, 13, 14, 16, 33, 99, 101, 107
Neustadt, 119
Ney, Michel, Duke of Elchingen, Prince of the Moscowa: defeats the enemy rear guard at Valutino, 24; welcomes Fezensac, 37; defends Vyazma, 57; defense of Dorogobuzh, 60–62; protects Dnieper passage, 64; defends Smolensk, 70–73; at the battle of Krasnii, 77–78; leads retreat, 78–80; replaces the Duke of Reggio, 96; his attitude toward death, 99–100; resumes command of the rear guard, 110; defends Kovno, 116; his opinion of Fezensac, 129; mentioned, 22, 32, 38, 60, 66, 75, 82, 85, 86, 87, 90, 95, 109, 111, 113, 114, 118, 119, 120, 121, 125
Noailles, M. Alfred de, 12, 99

Index

Novogrodeck, 7
Nogat Island, 122, 123

Oldenburg, 3
Orsha, 15, 21, 22, 70, 74, 75, 86, 89, 90
Oshmyani, 103
Ostrovno, 16
Oudinot, Nicolas-Charles. *See* Reggio, Duke of

Pelleport, M., 38, 116
Pernet, M., 11
Perushkovo, 40
Pillkahlen, 119
Platov, General, 81, 84, 85
Pleshchenitsy, 102
Plock, 121
Pnevo, 65
Podolsk, 52
Polotsk, 14, 17, 67
Poniatowski, Prince, 134
Posen, 4, 5, 124, 125
Postvia-Dvor, 60

Rapp, General, 124
Rasasno, 22
Razout, General, 38, 61, 62, 71, 78
Reggio, Nicolas-Charles Oudinot, Duke of, 17, 91, 92, 96, 99, 102
Richard, General, 76
Riga, 17, 19, 25
Roslavl, 50
Rostopchin, Governor, 40, 41
Rouchat, M., 64
Rykonti, 113

Saint-Denis, 13
Saint-Jean d'Acre, 24
Saint Petersburg, 8, 14
Salamanca, battle of, 30
Saliau, 119
Seminov Convent, 51
Semlevo, 28
Sheremetev, Count, 44
Shklov, 15
Sienno, 15
Sirokovich, 80

Index

Slopnevo, 64
Smolensk: occupation of, 22–24; retreat through, 69–70; defense of, 71–73; mentioned, 15, 16, 17, 19, 20, 21, 25, 26, 27, 46, 50, 54, 60, 69, 74, 89, 90
Smorgon, 103
Spandau, 126
Stary-Bykhov, 15
Stelton, 124
Stettin, 126

Talmont, M. de, 12
Tarutino, 53
Thorn, 5, 121
Tilsit, 7, 118, 119, 121, 124
Tolochin, 90
Tormasov, General, 6, 17, 67
Tula, 43
Tver, 40, 46

Ukholody, 93

Valutino, 24, 25
Valuyevo, 29
Velishchevo, 28
Vely, 17
Vereya, 46, 54
Veselovo, 93, 95, 97
Vileika, 102
Villeblanche, M. de, 69
Vilna: importance of, 9; retreat through, 107–109; mentioned, 5, 7, 8, 10, 12, 13, 19, 90, 95, 98, 99, 103
Vinkovo, 48
Vitebsk, 12, 14, 16, 17, 18, 19, 20, 22
Vladimir, 40, 43, 44
Volhynia, 6
Vyazma, 27, 28, 56, 57, 58, 59

Warsaw, 9, 121
Wengrov, 121
Wittgenstein, General, 14, 17, 67, 91, 92, 95, 97, 102
Wrede, General de, 102
Württemberg, Eugene, Prince of, 32, 37

Yorck, General, 124, 125

Index

Zayonschek, 134
Zembin, 98, 100
Zhizhmory, 112, 113

www.ingramcontent.com/pod-product-compliance
Lightning Source LLC
Chambersburg PA
CBHW020804160426
43192CB00006B/438